# MORE GROUSE FEATHERS

# More
# Grouse Feathers

BY BURTON L. SPILLER

*AUTHOR OF GROUSE FEATHERS*

ILLUSTRATED BY

LYNN BOGUE HUNT

Introduction by H. G. Tapply

CROWN PUBLISHERS, INC., NEW YORK

TO THOSE KINDRED SOULS

WHO HAVE CROWNED

THE RUFFED GROUSE

KING

THIS BOOK IS DEDICATED

# INTRODUCTION

This is the fourth and last of the books Burton L. Spiller wrote for publication by the old Derrydale Press. *Grouse Feathers,* the first, appeared in 1935; then came *Thoroughbred* in 1936, *Firelight* in 1937, and *More Grouse Feathers* in 1938. Copies of these old classics are rare today, as only 950 copies of each were printed, and they are treasured by collectors who cheerfully pay as much as $100 for one in good-to-mint condition.

Some say *Grouse Feathers* is Burt's best book; others believe *More Grouse Feathers* may be the better of the two. But there are so few of us who have had the opportunity to read them both it's hard to make a judgment—if indeed it is possible to do so.

Now Crown Publishers has made both available again in facsimile editions that faithfully reproduce the original Derrydale Press pages with their superb Lynn Bogue Hunt drawings, and it will be a joy to see the two volumes side by side on the bookshelf. Judge them as best you can. As far as I am concerned, one is as great as the other.

Burt is also the author of *Drummer in the Woods,* a collection of grouse-shooting stories he wrote for various outdoor magazines over the years, and a boy's adventure book, *Northland Castaways.* His short stories have appeared in *Cosmopolitan* and the old *Saturday Evening Post* and, of course, in most of the major sporting publications. He has also written plays and a vast quantity of poetry—very good poetry, too.

Yet he is by trade a blacksmith.

[ v ]

Burton Lowell Spiller was born on December 21, 1886, in Portland, Maine, where his father had a smithy. When Burt was eight the Spiller family moved to the little seacoast town of Wells, south of Portland, where his father taught him how to shoe horses. In 1911 he married Mildred Moulton, daughter of the owner of the town's general store, and moved to East Rochester, New Hampshire, where their daughter Ainslie was born. There he practiced blacksmithing for a while, then worked for nineteen years as a welder and machine fixer in a local woolen mill. When Pearl Harbor happened he helped to build submarines at Portsmouth Navy Yard in Kittery, Maine.

Hammering on machinery days and on an old Oliver typewriter nights, trout fishing in the spring and hunting grouse and woodcock and deer in the fall still wasn't enough to keep him fully occupied. In 1935 Burt began growing gladioli, harvesting as many as fifty thousand bulbs a year and developing several new varieties that were listed in the prestigious North American Gladiolus Registry. At odd times he made violins, beautifully crafted instruments of mellow tone and flawless workmanship.

As you can see, one way or another Burt managed to keep busy. Yet he accomplished all these things in only six days a week, for he was, and still is, a devout Baptist and Sunday was always set aside for the church. To my certain knowledge he never hunted on the Sabbath, although Sunday hunting has always been permitted in New Hampshire. In all the fourteen years we gunned together I can't remember ever hearing him utter even so mild an oath as "damn" or "hell" (unlike some of the characters in his stories who occasionally used these expletives), nor have I known him to touch a drop of spirituous liquor. Often we hunted in driving rain, early snowstorms, and bitter cold and never did he mention discomfort or suggest quitting early.

According to my hunting log, our last day's hunt together was on October 31, 1964. Sometime during the day Burt fell heavily while crossing a stone wall and cracked two ribs. It is typical of him that he said nothing of it, for fear of spoiling my fun. He hunted in pain till dusk—at close to age seventy-eight, mind you—and we made a date to hunt again the following Saturday. By then, however, the injury had become too painful to hide, and he told me what had happened. So he sat in the car while I put the dog through a few covers, but my heart wasn't in it.

The ribs have long since healed and Burt still lives with his daughter Ainslie in the old white house on the main street of East Rochester, next to the Baptist church. I drop in on him occasionally—as recently as last week, as a matter of fact—so we can refresh our memories as to certain incredible shots we have made or, even more incredibly, missed, and which dog it was that pointed the bird that got done in, or made its miraculous escape, and my, how the grouse feathers fly.

Too bad you can't sit in with us sometime, but here's a book with more grouse feathers that you'll enjoy as much.

H. G. Tapply

East Alton, New Hampshire
April 1972

# MORE GROUSE FEATHERS

# CHAPTER I

LIFE, I feel, cannot be accurately measured by the ticking of a clock, or by the arbitrary numbering of a period of years.

My own, I find as I review it, is roughly divided into periods of sevens. I can recall no essential change in myself as six of my birthdays rolled into the limbo of forgotten things, but I do know that on the seventh a metamorphosis took place, in which I emerged from the chrysalis of babyhood and became a boy. The exact type of boy is still a matter of family record, but I see no reason for making it public, and save for certain highlights which I may choose to recall, the rest must remain forever locked in the archives of an all-too-well-remembered past.

Although my first seven years were devoted largely to things far removed from sport, they undoubtedly did serve to direct my fancy toward the track it would presently follow, for it was a dull evening indeed when someone did not drop in to discuss with Dad some phase of hunting, and more often than not the emphasis was laid on grouse.

There was, too, a rather well-stocked library dealing with hunting and fishing: serious, technical stuff, and well-thumbed books of American fiction. It was the latter which interested me most, especially one ponderous green-covered volume entitled, *The Bear Hunters of the Rocky Mountains*. I must have been a precocious child so far as reading was concerned, for I went through it from cover to cover, not once, but many times, until I could almost repeat it from memory. How old I was when I first tackled it I do not know, but I am positive I never saw it after I was eight, for we moved then, and the book, either purposely or otherwise, was lost in the shuffle. I wish I might see it again. For just one evening I would like to renew my acquaintance with Harold and Rodney, and toil with them across the long, long trail from the Pacific to the Atlantic. Those were the grand old days when men were men—and boys were inevitably heroes. It was a dull page indeed whereon the life of some member of the party did not hang precariously in the balance.

Bears and fallen logs were everywhere, and the chances were at least two to one that if a fellow took a running jump over one of the latter he would land fairly upon the sleeping forms of a whole family of the former. Never before were so many bears crowded between the covers of one book. It seems impossible there could have been any room left for Indians, but they were there, whole tribes of them, making the air ring with their war-whoops, and filling the nights with terror.

How I would like to meet poor old Dennis once more,

[ 2 ]

that I might inquire concerning his cough. A tricky and uncertain thing, that cough, for it was set on a hair trigger. He might carry it around for days on end without jarring it loose, but let the little band start wiggling its way through a redskin camp and it became an entirely different matter. Upon the utter silence of the night it would burst forth, as startling as a pistol shot, bringing the savages to their feet *en masse*, and from then until the close of the chapter blood flowed like water.

I suppose I would get many a laugh from it now, but I took it seriously enough then, and like many another trifling thing it had something to do with the shaping of my destiny. I was a potential hunter before that well-worn book ever found its way into my hands, but before I had finished reading it for the first time I was an avowed one, my life dedicated to the ever-new thrill of following some dim woodland trail.

Until I was seven, fishing played no part in my life. It was there in the background for me to feed upon, but as yet it had not impressed itself upon my consciousness. Save for some personally conducted excursions to the brook behind the house, where with a bent pin and a bit of thread I played upon the childish credulity of a school of minnows, I had looked upon fish with disdain. Compared to grouse —and silvertips—they were not worthy of consideration,

[ 3 ]

but an event occurred which forever changed my mind concerning them. It thrilled me at the time, although there was little of pleasure in the experience, and it left its mark upon me. I am glad now that it did, for while nothing has ever occupied the particular niche in my life that upland shooting fills, yet fishing has somehow rounded it out and made of many an otherwise drab day a bright and happy one.

Our milkman was a fisherman, a combination of vocation and avocation to which I am fundamentally opposed. I am not averse to mixing business with pleasure, and I accord to every man that privilege, but I do think a milkman should use a bit more discretion in his choice of pastimes.

I do not know who planned the excursion, or whether my presence was due to sober deliberation or a hasty afterthought, but I remember sitting in a high-wheeled carriage behind a plodding horse, with the milkman on one side of me and my father on the other, an assortment of jointed rods rolled in a horse blanket beneath our feet, and a gallon or two of milk sloshing about in a half-filled can on the floor behind us.

We came presently to higher country, a winding wood road, and at last a lake, encircled by rocks which, to me at least, seemed gigantic. What a strange thing is memory.

I have not the slightest recollection of what we did with the horse. He passed out of my life when we climbed down from the wagon, but the taste of that milk is still warm upon my lips, and I can see again the dipperful they gave me, with golden chunks of butter floating around on top in mute testimony of the vigorous churning it had received en route.

The picture blurs, and when it comes once more into sharp focus I see myself standing on a perfect tabletop of rock that rises from the very waters of the lake. The waters are a rich, sky-blue, and they whisper and purl invitingly about the base of the rock as I toss a bit of shale over the edge and watch it disappear into the depths.

There are three rods. Even my rudimentary arithmetic can prove that, for the milkman is assembling one, my father is threading line through the guides of another, and one more is lying on the rock between us. I know without asking that one of them is for me, but I am not thrilled at the prospect. I am not yet a fisherman, therefore I regard them skeptically and with a bit of awe.

My conception of them, both then and now, is that they were large rods. Subsequent events only served to strengthen my belief, but when Dad placed one of them in my hands I found its weight far exceeded my expectations. Only by leaning backward and stretching my hands far apart could I hold it erect for more than a moment at a time, and even then I feared to stir lest my feet describe an arc in the air behind me.

Acting upon orders, although much against my inclination, I twisted cautiously about and dropped the baited hook and half the line over the edge. Lowering the rod relieved the strain somewhat, but it was still very heavy. I permitted it to dip still deeper, then raised it aloft in an effort to find some happy medium of balance that would ease the ache in my arms and wrists. The action was highly effective. I imagine that in some water-worn grotto far beneath my feet an old bass had found a retreat to his liking, and the bobbing bait must have attracted his fancy, for my aimless twitching of the rod was brought to a sudden and dramatic halt.

So small I was, and so fearful of getting too close to the edge, that I saw neither telltale rush nor warning boiling of the waters. At one moment I was standing there, already tired and more than slightly bored, and in the next instant the rod was bent so far down that its tip was under water, while I, yelling mightily for one so young, braced far back and clung to the distorted bit of bamboo with an energy born of my desperate need. There was in my mind not the slightest doubt that I would be drawn bodily from the rock, but with what power I possessed I fought to delay the moment. To this day I do not know what made me cling to the rod, but cling I did, with every last ounce that was in me, reserving only enough energy to send out an occasional and frantic plea for reinforcements.

No big-game fisherman was ever so harried as I, so wrenched and twisted and buffeted about; and none ever had a more appreciative gallery, for the milkman flanked me on one side and my father on the other, shouting words of encouragement and lending me their moral support; but neither of them so much as lifted a little finger to give me the physical help for which I prayed.

There was, I am sure, something primal and brutish in the encounter, as there must ever be when two creatures of the wild are engaged in a battle in which life is the reward and death the penalty. In each of us burned the fierce will to live, and to each of us it must have lent added power, for while the bass jumped and splashed, and darted hither and yon in a frenzied effort to escape, some unsuspected reserve of stamina within me gave me the strength to hang on.

I am glad now that they did not help me, even though I begged, entreated and implored them to do so. It was my fight, and as interested as they were in it, each had the good judgment to withhold his hand and let me win or lose on my own merit. I am sorry for the boy who does not have a father like mine. I am sorry for the one who is so petted and

[ 7 ]

pampered and mollycoddled that he runs crying for protection at the first hint of adversity. I am sorry, too, for the one who has never had the opportunity to get out and pit his skill against nature in the raw.

It must have been a great battle, for blurred though it is by its own violence and the passage of time, the memory of those aching arms lingers with me yet. I suppose, too, the bass was not as large as I like to imagine him, or I would never have won; but win I eventually did, for with a superhuman effort I shortened my grip on the rod, and managed somehow or other to drag the monster up on the rocks beside me, where the milkman pounced upon him with a fervor equalled only by the manner in which my father fell upon me.

I was engulfed with praise, the gasping form of the vanquished was held aloft for my inspection, and I was informed, solemnly, by both parties, that I was a fisherman born; but I fear I missed the fine glow which I have later come to associate with the landing of a good fish. The thing had not been of my choosing. It had been forced upon me more or less against my will, and the relief I felt at my escape far outweighed any satisfaction I might have felt over winning the battle. It did, however, leave a mark upon me, burned rather deeply into my soul, and if I have been guilty of forgetting my feathered friends for a time during the long days of summer, the blame may justly be placed on that first black bass of the long ago.

Our home was in the suburbs of Maine's queen city, but I would give much to find again, for just one fall, a place where grouse were as plentiful as they were in the vast and mysterious woodland which came down to meet our little field. The brook in which I had fished for minnows originated somewhere within its depths, and some inborn sense of woodsmanship told me that I could never become lost so long as I followed its erratic wanderings, hence it was not long before my quest for adventure led me into what was, for me at least, a forbidden domain.

I shall never forget the thrill I felt when I pushed for the first time into that great, cool silence. I cannot recall that it seemed either new to me or strange. It was as though I had known it always, and yet it filled me with awe and reverence and an ineffable satisfaction. I know now that the blood of wanderers flows in my veins: that I am a product not many generations removed from a line of forebears to whom the far horizons ever looked the fairest; but at that time I only knew that the murmuring brook and the whispering of the wind among the treetops filled me at once with both a great yearning and a great content.

Curiously enough, I still know the same sensation at times. Only last summer, while on a canoe trip through the interior of Nova Scotia, while portaging from one lake to another, we came into virgin forest. It was like entering a great cathedral. High overhead the interlaced branches forever barred the sunlight, and in the pleasant shade beneath them neither creeping plant nor shrub marred the velvety smoothness of the age-old carpet of fallen needles. As far as eye could reach, the mammoth columns arose, serenely keeping their sentinel vigil which had been centuries long. Forgetful alike of the canoe-laden guide who strode along before me, the portage, and the lake yet to be crossed before the coming of darkness, I slipped my pack, let it fall unnoticed to the ground, and knew again that old awe and reverence which I had felt on that other day so long ago.

But although I still experience the thrill at times, it lacks something of the tense excitement and expectancy that it had in the other days, for that neighboring wood was peopled alike by forest folk and strange creatures of my own imagining. Rabbits scuttled away at my approach, the pound of their feet coming back to me long after they had vanished from view. Grouse hammered up before me, shattering the murmuring silence with the roar of their wings, and startling me anew each time, even though their soft twitterings had warned me that the take-off was imminent.

It was here I encountered my first mother grouse with her brood. Rounding a bend in the trail along the bank, I came squarely upon them. The tiny chicks, not yet half the size of my chubby fist, darted out from under foot and instantly were magically hidden among the fallen leaves; but a brown bundle of fury was upon me, crying shrilly, buffeting my thinly clad legs with her wings, and pecking at them so savagely that it set not only the blood but my feet to running.

I have been beaten thousands of times by ruffed grouse since then, although never again so literally. I recall now that my hasty retreat was the result of good judgment rather than fear, and although my legs smarted for a time, I cherished no resentment, but only a warm appreciation of the plucky mother, and a realization that here indeed was a quarry worthy of all the praise I had heard accorded it.

It was in this enchanted land that I met my first Indian, although I failed to recognize him for what he was when he materialized out of the forest. I had built a wigwam not far from the edge of the wood. It was a masterpiece of craftsmanship, fully three feet in height, constructed chiefly of a fallen log, some scraggy poles and a few evergreen branches; but it was so strategically placed that by lying curled within it I could keep one wary eye on the house while with the other I surveyed the forest behind me.

Into this solitude my Indian came, an axe in his hand, and a bundle of basket-stock upon his back. Had the axe been a tomahawk, or had he worn the prescribed head-dress of feathers I think I would have recognized him for what he was; but although he was more than a little dark of complexion, I ascribed it (and rightly, too, I still think) as much to dirt as to any inherited coloration. In this we had a common bond, so I peered out at him stolidly from my place of concealment, and knew not so much as a single warning flutter of apprehension.

He spotted me instantly, threw down his bundle, and invited me to come forth. A bit chagrined that my retreat had been so easily discovered, I complied, and thus began a friendship from which, short though it was, I profited immensely. He saw the weakness of my bivouac at a glance, and with a dozen strokes of his axe lopped off half that many poles, set them in approved wigwam fashion, bound their tops together with a bit of brush, and gave me a practical demonstration of how the primal redskin wove his domicile of evergreen branches. I had labored over my structure for days, but in fifteen minutes he had completed one that was a comparative palace.

To me, he was only an entrancing stranger, but some intuitive sense told me that it might be well to keep the matter of our acquaintance a secret. I managed to do so for a week or more, but one day he brought me a perfectly wonderful bow and half a dozen arrows, the former shrewdly designed to fit my slender physique, and the latter so nicely balanced and feathered that their flight was unbelievably smooth. It was a magnificent gift, but my pride in its ownership proved to be my undoing. I exhibited it at the house, and the result was one which I might have readily foreseen. I was put through a rigorous third degree, and reluctantly I told all.

Hitherto the fates had been kind to me, but now they ceased to smile. In the West the Apaches were still making occasional forays, and the memory of Custer's massacre was still green. My Indian, it developed, was merely one of the nomadic Passamaquoddy tribe that had always been friendly with the whites, but that made no difference. In the eyes of my parents he was a savage, and therefore not to be trusted. I don't know whether they expected he would scalp me, but I was forbidden to go into the woods alone, and saw him no more. In fact, now that I pause to consider the matter, I do not recall ever seeing my brush wigwam again after that ill-fated afternoon.

I had been taught obedience, but the smell of that rotting leaf-mold was in my nostrils, and nothing could again keep my feet forever on city streets. There was, I discovered, a vast difference between the letter and the spirit of a law. That prohibited bit of wood was not the only one in the territory, and it was not long before I was exploring newer and more enticing trails. A neighbor's son, some two or three years my senior, unwittingly furnished the means. He was as harum-scarum a youth as it has ever been my good fortune to know, but he had the saintly demeanor of Little Lord Fauntleroy, and had been held aloft many a time by distracted parents, mine included, as the perfect pattern of manhood in the making.

My bow and arrow proved to be the magic key to the door of his good graces, and for the remainder of the summer he cultivated my friendship as assiduously as ever country swain wooed village belle. Precocious far beyond his years, I was yet his match, for I played the cards which were mine with an instinctive good judgment that even yet fills me with wonder. It was not my companionship but my implements of war that he coveted, and I was quick to realize the power that was mine so long as I retained possession of them. Resisting all his blandishments and every offer to trade, I yet managed to appear always on the point of doing so, and thus was privileged to enjoy many a woodland ramble in his company that would have been forbidden otherwise.

It was this friendship of ours that paved the way to my first planned campaign to reduce a cock grouse to the essential fundamentals of a partridge pie, and but for an altogether human trait on his part, which cropped out at the crucial moment, the plan might have succeeded.

In the course of our wanderings we had found a log on which a vainglorious cock daily performed a series of post-season drummings. The hollow beat of his wings had attracted us from afar, and after many disappointments we were at last able to creep close enough to watch him in the act. I believe now that the interesting action is pretty generally understood, but the prevailing opinion then (and I still encounter it occasionally) was that the boastful fellow was dependent upon a *hollow* log that would reverberate like an African tom-tom when he beat upon it. Obviously such a supposition is erroneous, for even in the years when grouse are scarce there are not enough hollow logs to go around, and if they were lying there by millions not one of them would produce that echoing drum-beat.

Our grouse, all unaware of our approach, strode the length of his half-rotten, moss-grown log, with all the majestic arrogance of a parading turkey-gobbler. His tail was lifted and spread to its fullest extent. His wings were stretched so stiffly downward that the long flight-feathers separated and their tips brushed the log beside him. His head was held high aloft, and the blue-black ruff at the sides of his neck stood sharply out. He pirouetted grandly for a moment, then stood more rigidly erect and brought his wings together before him with the quickness of light. Without relaxing the tenseness of his body in the slightest degree he repeated the movement after a momentary interval, and then again and again, in ever increasing tempo, until the wings were an indistinguishable blur, and the booming beat had softened into the rapid roll of a snare drum. He relaxed then, shook his feathers into place, listened a moment and then resumed his strutting.

To me, he was the essence of all things desirable, and my companion shared my belief; but to get close enough to end forever his boasting challenge was beyond our most painstaking effort, as we speedily learned when we tried to approach within arrow range, for he was off in thundering flight before we had moved half the length of our bodies toward him. Thus began a siege that lasted for weeks, and which gave birth at last to a grand idea.

My model youth may have been held up as a paragon of virtue in the neighborhood, but it developed that the feeling was not generally shared by his relatives. He had been one of the leading participants in a gunpowder plot which had necessitated not only a day's work by the village glazier upon the kitchen windows in the parental abode, but the purchase of a new cookstove as well. Because of that, and other events of a related nature, an embargo had been placed upon such munitions and firearms as the structure boasted; and to be certain that no attempt would be made on his part to run the blockade, they had been locked in a windowless cupboard, and the key so effectively hidden that not even his prying nose could smell out its place of concealment.

It required no great acumen on our parts to realize that we needed a weapon of considerably longer range than my diminutive arrows; but how to acquire it was, for the time at least, something of a problem, for while my parents had yet to learn the caution which came to them later, our gun cabinet was also locked, and the key was in my father's pocket. How to acquire a gun was a problem that defied our powers of solution until I chanced to remember the revolver in the top drawer of a bureau in the room which my parents occupied.

The inspiration was a happy one, and I could not have thought of it at a more propitious time, for Dad was at his place of business, while Mother, her mind at ease because I was in the competent keeping of the model boy, had taken advantage of the moment to make a social call somewhere (as I afterward learned) in the immediate vicinity.

A coal hole and an unlocked cellar door made the entrance all too easy, and we were presently standing again in the back yard, with a pearl-handled target revolver in his hands, and a half-filled box of tallow-coated and blunt-nosed cartridges in mine.

It was then that the human trait to which I referred stepped in to mar the unparalleled smoothness of the primrose path we trod. Like any true sportsman, no sooner was the gun in his hands than he had an overmastering impulse to try it. Logical enough in itself, for no one should risk a shot at game without first proving his weapon, it was yet ill advised. While we resided in what we were pleased to call the suburbs of the city, it was not truly the most rural of communities, and even I had sense enough to realize that a sudden burst of gunfire on that lazy September afternoon would cause more than one inquisitive head to be thrust from a hastily opened window.

Whether I objected I do not recall, but I remember surrendering the cartridge box and watching in open-mouthed admiration while, with deft, sure fingers, he flicked the gate open, shoved the six cartridges home in their respective places in the cylinder, and looked about for a target that would call for the best that was in him.

Since that eventful afternoon I have hunted with all manner of marksmen, and have come to believe that the lucky one is Fortune's favorite child. Although the law of averages is all against him, I have seen some truly remarkable shots made by the rankest of rank tyros, and I know at least two of them who do it with a frequency that is really marvellous. My youthful prototype was similarly blessed by the gods.

On a little eminence but slightly removed from the house, stood our wooden pump, its handle pointing skyward as though, metaphorically, it had already thrown up its hands in horror; but its mute plea was wasted. My companion whipped the gun up from his hip, and while it was still rising pulled the trigger. I have seen Buffalo Bill shoot when he was at the height of his career. I have watched the cold precision of Captain Johnny Baker, the inspired exhibitions of Annie Oakley and the studied perfection of the Topperweins, but they all lacked the heaven-born something with which my friend was endowed.

The first shot struck the pump fairly low down, as vital shots should, perforated both the cylinder and the leather-lined box, and whined away into the distance like an angry hornet. The nearby wood flung back an almost instantaneous echo, but, quick as it was, it could only blend and merge with the sound of the second report. That bullet hit the curve of the iron spout, ricocheted sharply, passed through a window in the henhouse (which chanced to be closed at the time) and ceased its tumultuous flight by imbedding itself deeply in the opposite wall. No thin board could have stopped it so easily, but in the course of its brief

journey through the structure it had encountered a raised
and lath-slatted dais where, at times, certain male members
of the flock were groomed for exhibition at the State Fair.
The bullet passed through two of the laths, and also, I regret to say, through the meatier portion of a Black Minorca
rooster who chanced to be occupying the interior at the
time, thus forever ending whatever ambitions either he or
my dad may have secretly cherished.

These things were ascertained later, by a process of de-
duction, for I think that each of us entertained a growing
conviction that this preliminary warming-up must of necessity be an exceedingly limited one. The next shot was
unpremeditated, for so great was his haste that, in looking
about for some more-difficult target, he discharged the
piece accidentally; but his luck was of the sort that has
more than once broken the bank at Monte Carlo. A blue
flowerpot, in which a late geranium bloomed, stood on one
of the lower steps that led up to the house; as the unexpected shot rang out, it leaped convulsively and collapsed
in a thousand shattered fragments.

It has been my lifelong regret that I was not privileged
to know what would have been the result if the three remaining cartridges had been fired, but at that moment there
came to our ears a strained, feminine cry, and I looked
about to see my mother, her skirts raised and whipping

stiffly back with the wind of her flight, bearing down upon us from across the street.

It is at once both my delight and my despair to see with what lightning-like rapidity a great mind may work in a crisis. The youth whose sterling character I had been prayerfully implored to emulate, hesitated by not so much as a fraction of a second, but thrust the revolver, still cocked, into one of my nerveless hands, the cartridge box into the other, and departed with a celerity only equaled by the passage of light.

Notwithstanding the affirmative opinion of many eminent criminologists, I am still opposed to the meting out of capital punishment on the strength of circumstantial evidence alone. I know what it means to have the prosecution pile up point on point until the innocent victim's spirit is bowed beneath the accumulated weight. I know the hopeless feeling that comes to one when he realizes that his reiterated protestations of innocence are not believed. I know the bitterness of realizing that the real culprit is going his unperturbed way while the innocent bystander is languishing behind prison bars, for it was I who paid the penalty to the last full measure.

I quote these events neither idly nor because of the painful memories they recall, but because they had a direct bearing upon my life. Of all the dream creatures that had

peopled my childish mind, grouse had always been para-
mount. They had occupied the place of honor most frequently, both in and out of season, and there were endless
discussions to which I was privileged at times to listen, concerning grouse and their ways. As my mind goes back to
those lost days I am forced to admit frankly that I was far
from being a model youth; but I was, I believe, a typical
young American, for in no other nationality is the love for
the wild so firmly implanted. It is our racial heritage. That
ineffable urge which drove our forefathers to take up the
battle against the wilderness crops out pretty regularly
among their offspring, and creates anew in each generation
a problem which fathers must face.

My quest for weapons was an entirely natural instinct,
and one which a majority of my youthful countrymen
share. That I found them and learned to use them with no
more serious results than I may chance to recall, was largely
due to the graciousness of Lady Luck. I think it had always
been an accepted fact in the family that I would become a
hunter, but the schooling I should have received to fit me
for that absorbing pastime was deferred until that nebulous
day when I should be both old enough and big enough.

I know of no more common fault among parents. No
matter how zealously guarded a boy's life may be, the time
will almost certainly come when he will either handle fire-

arms, or find himself in the company of other boys who are doing so, and in either case his chance of emerging from the affair in a watertight condition is in direct proportion to the familiarity the participants have with the weapon. But I digress.

That first brief bout of mine with Dad's target revolver was far from satisfactory, and by some queer process of reasoning, or lack of it, I looked upon the weapon with disfavor, blaming it, rather than my own imprudence, for my inclination to remain standing for a long time thereafter. Painful though the affair was, it was not without its benefits, and especially to the animal kingdom. Our campaign against the grouse was abandoned, and, so far, at least, as we were concerned, he was left to send his booming challenge echoing through the woodland as freely as his fancy prompted.

In *Grouse Feathers* I made brief mention of a trip with my father into Maine's north country, but I feel I did not sufficiently stress the influence it had upon me. Previous to that time my conception had been that men hunted only for sport, but here we came in contact with individuals who made it their business. Childlike, I saw but one aspect of the practice, and that, of course, was the glamorous side. To be able to follow game trails for days on end, and to subsist by doing so, became all at once the pinnacle of all

[ 23 ]

things desirable. I did not know until long afterward that I had been born a generation too late, therefore when we returned to the haunts of civilization I was fired with a new resolve, and one that had a marked bearing on my life for years to come. That my ambition was not fulfilled does not matter. In my pursuit of it I found other things which brought me happiness.

Not so long ago a business man said to me (and his words held a significance that many a young man would do well to heed): "If I could live my life over again there are two things which I would do. I would learn to play a violin, and I would try to learn to be a good shot."

That was the order of their importance in his mind. There was no thought of correcting the mistakes he had undoubtedly made in his business, no yearning for greater wealth or executive power than had been his, but only a great regret that he had missed from life the things he most desired, and which might have been his for the taking.

I suppose, though, that chance plays its part in even the best-ordered lives, and I am sure that it played an important part in mine. When Dad's health failed, and he broke the shackles and moved to that country farm, he made a choice for which I shall never cease to bless him. It not only brought back his health but it opened a veritable fairyland to me. Acre upon acre of tilled land stretched away on a gentle southern slope to merge at last into an expanse of wood that swept in a great, new-moon crescent far away on either side. Within that crescent lay thousands of acres of marshland, some of it tide swept, but a gratifying portion of it protected by long dykes, and cut by numerous waterways and springy shores, where curlew and plover and all manner of greater and lesser yellowlegs congregated in fabulous numbers. At either end of the marsh a river ran, winding in and out, between banks cut perpendicularly down through the peat-like deposit of untold centuries. In the abrupt bends where the force of the current was broken, beds of eelgrass grew, and here, as well as in the sweeter waters of the marshes, ducks fed in the spring and fall in numbers to defy the imagination of the New England youth of today.

Beyond the marsh lay rolling sand dunes, while beyond them lay the beach, curved as were the woods and marshes behind it. Two hundred yards in width at dead low tide, it was as smooth and hard as a race track. Thousands of times I have seen its two-mile length spotted by flock after flock of all the lesser shore birds, and with a pretty generous sprinkling of the greater ones as well.

A little way off-shore several groups of rocks thrust themselves up from the ocean's floor, just out of gun range even when the tide was at its lowest; and it was there that the migrating geese found safe refuge. I have never known anything more exasperating, for I have often seen them sit calmly while I waded out to my boot-tops and beyond, and look at one another and gabble among themselves as though they considered it the funniest joke in the world.

It was a happy time, but even then the oldtimer was sighing for the lost days of his youth when ducks were plentiful, or when he could lie in his blind before a baited bit of ground and kill a backload of passenger pigeons at one shot. The pigeons had gone, and the waterfowl and shore birds were on their way before I was commissioned for active service, but even so, I helped to speed their departure, for I was soon elected to take full charge of the munitions department, and for several weeks each spring and fall I had my hands quite literally full.

Among the various other items in the war chest, were thirty 10-gauge shells, presumably of brass, although they were so tarnished by time, powder smoke and salt water that my identification of the metal is largely a matter of conjecture. Day after day I would load them to their muzzles, and night after night, when the chores were done, Dad would stuff them in his pockets, shoulder Old Betsy and go down to the marshes.

Lying in bed, with my face, like that of a good Mohammedan, turned toward the east, I would prop my eyes open and wait for the barrage to start, for I had an artist's pride in my work, and it afforded me no end of satisfaction to hear those echoing reports. I suppose it may seem like a strange sort of lullaby to some, but I have never heard sweeter music that the muffled report of duck guns on a distant marsh, and I know that others share my feeling. I remember "Old George"; many a wide-eyed hour I spent in his immaculate kitchen while I listened to the stories he had to tell of the days when he was a "young feller."

Directly above his spotless kitchen-stove the ceiling was perforated by hundreds of round, smoothly cut holes to which little flecks of plaster still clung. They excited my curiosity, for they looked suspiciously like bullet holes, and when I inquired concerning them Old George rather shamefacedly explained their origin. His rheumatism had long since barred him from the field, but the yearning for the acrid smell of burned powder was something that would never die within him so long as he drew breath. When the crisp fall evenings came and the yearning grew irresistible, he would let the kitchen fire die down while he prepared for bed. When it had cooled sufficiently he would hobble out, throw in a bundle of kindling, set five revolver cartridges one after another in a line from the front cover well back to the center of the stove.

Then he would creep back to bed; only it was no

longer a bed, for once more Old George was crouching in a duck blind, warmed again by the fires of youth as he waited for the whistle of phantom wings. Out of the darkness they would come in myriad hosts, swinging in across the broad marshes, circling high overhead, or sliding down on drooping pinions to hover for a moment before they pitched into the eelgrass beds.

"Now!" The crackle of the fire was not unlike the stiff bending of frosty garments when a man went into action, and if Old George had gauged it to a nicety there would come a report from the first of the five shells, and ducks would come tumbling down into the quiet waters.

As the fire took hold and sucked back under the remaining shells the action quickened. Sometimes he pulled a snappy double, but not often, for the moment was too sweet to be hurried, and he was back once more in the days when one must be frugal with his ammunition. So he waited, picking his shots, and when the last shell was gone he would lie peacefully, the sweet powder smoke once more in his lungs, and his spirit filled with a great content.

I thought Old George a bit "queer," not knowing that he was but dreaming the dreams of every hunter in all the world: for who among us is so young that he does not paint a thousand fanciful pictures of the morrow—or who so old that he does not live again his glorious yesterdays?

So I, too, lay in my bed and listened to the music of those distant shots, and fell asleep with the comforting assurance that before long it would be my finger that was crooking around the trigger. Then, on the morrow, I would hurry home from school, seize those brass shells, drag out the ammunition box and once more cram them full for the evening fray. If ever the fates have been kind to me they most certainly were in those irresponsible days, for my lack of caution in handling that black powder was something to make the cold chills run up and down one's spine. More than once when giving the loaded shells a final inspection, I found that I had neglected to recap one or more of the number, and faced the problem of whether I should draw the charges, or take a chance on crowding a new primer home without taking that precaution. More than once, when time was pressing, I followed the latter course, until one day a primer exploded in an empty case, whereupon I decided on the safety-first policy to which I have since rigidly adhered.

Meanwhile, I was growing up, although far from fast enough to suit my impatient spirit, for it seemed the time would never come when I would be physically able to hold Old Betsy to my shoulder. But while I was barred from those nightly excursions to the marshes, I was occasionally accorded another privilege for which I was sincerely grateful. There were then, as now, a few hunters who shot only sitting grouse, and, to such, a "tree" dog was invaluable; but most wing shots could find all the shooting they wished without bothering with either pointer or setter. But because I begged to go along on those afternoons when Dad found it convenient to get away, I was accorded the privilege, with the proviso that I play dog, and beat the runs and hollows while he stood at some strategic point and intercepted such birds as came his way. It afforded me not too much of a thrill, but it did teach me something of the ways of grouse, and I know it was of immense value to me later when I began to handle dogs, for who better than I could understand the problems they had to face?

Yes, those years while I waited for my body to catch up with my mind were long ones, but there was all manner of fishing to be had, and while I knew it could never fill my life so completely as shooting would eventually do, it was yet an absorbing pursuit, and on several occasions was lifted to an even loftier plane. One such incident I recall as vividly as though it had happened within the hour.

Great-aunt Sophia was dead.

She had never been more than a name to me, but in a detached sort of way I felt that I owed her a debt of gratitude. It was quite considerate of her, I thought, to have timed it so I would win a midweek holiday. The funeral *cortège* would not arrive until noon, but aside from the discomfort of wearing a stiffly starched blouse and tight-fitting blue trousers, the day promised to be one of more than passing interest.

For a time the rooms occupied my attention. With their stiffly arranged chairs and fern-banked fireplaces, they seemed to have swelled perceptibly in size. There was also an unaccustomed flurry and bustling about in the kitchen, while the mingled odors of sliced meats and spicy sweetbreads impartially permeated the interior of both house and boy.

Several efforts to sample these culinary triumphs having met with a notable lack of success, the project was temporarily abandoned, and I fell to wandering aimlessly through the rooms once more, to the great annoyance of one Nora Collins, a freckled female whose one claim to distinction lay in the fact that she was generally accredited with being responsible for the existence of the greatest problem our town fathers had as yet been called upon to face: a red-headed and fascinatingly depraved youth of about my own age, who was customarily designated by the appellation "Kiko."

"Why don't the loikes of ye go out av doors and play?" she querulously inquired. "Sure, ye'd drive a body crazy wid your wanderin' about and kickin' up more dust than I could wipe off wid four hands. Why they kept you home from school is more than I know. Go on wid yourself, and kape out of a body's way. Mind that shirt waist, now. If ye get any dirt on it ye'll be gettin' a trowelin' too, most likely."

I thought her logic fundamentally sound, and so I went outside, edged through a rose arbor, passed behind the lilac bushes, and using a row of thrifty young grapevines for a screen, won my way at last to a corner of the shed and sanctuary from the all-seeing maternal eye that supervised affairs in the kitchen.

Then there was the orchard, the ground white with fallen petals, and overhead the ceaseless drone of bees feverishly working the last blossoms. The slope of the field next, with the lush grass already ankle-deep and splashed with the gold of dandelions. Then the river, winding lazily— and Kiko Collins, with cane pole and wire noose, snaring pickerel from among the lily pads.

I can see it again, clearly. The bamboo pole, its tip cut back to the size of my little finger for strength, the bright copper wire with its six-inch running noose, the pickerel sunning themselves in the shallows, so charmed by that glittering circle that they permit it to be slid back over their heads, or sometimes drifting lazily ahead to shove their snouts voluntarily through the fatal ring.

"Yay, Kike!" I call. "Your mother's up at our house, workin'. We're goin' to have a fun'ral. I bet you wish you were goin'."

"Don't neither!" Kiko disclaims even a passing interest in funerals. "Have all the fun'rals you want for all me." He garrotes another fish and heaves it far up on the bank. "Have one every day if you want. I'd rather go fishin'."

The picture lingers. Kiko, bare-legged and gallus-crossed, follows the marshy shore, while I, starched and ruffled, tread the firmer ground, yet manage to keep my course on an exact parallel with his. I see the narrowing stream, with its banks growing ever more abrupt, the trees leaning sharply out over the water—and then the grist mill, its roof gray with moss, its dam spanning the narrow gorge.

It is the noon hour. The miller is gone and the wheels have ceased their turning. The water, drawn down by the morning run, has exposed two feet of the upper portion of the dam. Steeply slanting, with its inch-thick coating of half-dried slime, it possesses a magnetic attraction that is well-nigh irresistible, but I remember my starches and refrain. The ten-inch plate, though, at the crest of the dam, is level and comparatively dry, a challenge to careful foot-work and steady brain. We walk the plate, Kiko in the lead, balancing himself with the pole while I follow with out-stretched arms.

[ 33 ]

Halfway across we pause and peer down the twenty-foot drop to the pool beneath. The grandfather of all trout is lying there, partly hidden by a jutting rock, but breathtakingly gigantic.

"Chris'mus!"

The ejaculation is Kiko's, and he at once begins exchanging the wire noose for a faded green line and generous hook. I wait with bated breath while he extracts two worms from his pocket, loops them on and lowers them reverently, a votive offering to his god.

Hope rises, then wanes. The god is disdainful and refuses even to glance at the delicacy, nor will Kiko's clever manipulation of it into a series of coy advances and terrified retreats cause the omnipotent one to change his mind.

A different lure is suggested and I mention frogs. Kiko agrees, so I go in search of one. Haste seems imperative and I neglect my foot work. I go down, crashingly, upon my back, but manage by a perfect miracle of good luck to secure a last moment grip on the plate. I roll over on my stomach, crawl back, and resume my interrupted way.

The frog is a green one with black stripes, and is active beyond all comparison. He has a predilection for muck and mire, but my determination is born of our urgent need, and he is carried to the sacrificial altar.

There is an argument as to proprietary rights but I am

fixed in my purpose and Kiko surrenders the rod. I impale the frog, which protests without avail, and lower him into the depths.

What follows is epochal, but the impression has always remained blurred. It is a human weakness. Only the observer on the heights may accurately record the conflict. The thrust and parry, and the clash of battle mercifully leave but superficial etchings on the memory of he who wields the sword. I recall a chaos of shoutings. Kiko's is high pitched and authoritative in its assurance of superior generalship, while mine is the equally vociferous expression of a feebler intellect gone happily mad.

Likewise there remains some faint impression of an Herculean struggle, of slippings and slidings, and of precarious balances regained after they had seemed irrevocably lost.

It ends at last. The picture comes into sharper focus, yet it is curiously restricted in area. The sun shines brighter, the grass grows greener, the world is fairer than I have ever known it, yet I move through the rosy light as one moves through an encompassing fog, my minute sphere the center of all existence, my one luminary the trout I hug to my bedraggled bosom.

In that same enveloping haze I move through the line of waiting carriages. I see the black horses and the blacker hearse, but they do not register on my consciousness. I move as a sleep-walker moves, actuated by a power over which I have no control.

The front gate stands ajar, symbolizing the portals which have opened for Great-aunt Sophia. I push through it and float up the graveled path. Pausing only to secure a firmer grip on my trout, and to thrust it a bit more forward that no first satisfying eyeful may be lost, I step inside the open front door.

No thespian who ever trod the boards achieved a greater entrance than mine. The bishop's voice faltered, and the prayer book slid to the floor from his nerveless fingers. He said, "Bless my soul!" quite audibly, and then a hushed and brooding silence fell on the assembled throng.

Poor Great-aunt Sophia! Doomed to go through life unheralded and unsung, her last supreme effort to gain recognition was to go unrewarded. A mud-besmirched urchin, holding aloft a fishy-smelling and sad-eyed trout, held the center of the stage.

Time, mercifully, has again blurred much which subsequently transpired. I recall a startled shriek, in a voice that was suggestive of (although wholly unlike) my mother's, and then a long, tremulous exhalation of multitudinous breaths, but there is no sequence to the impressions which still linger, until that moment when I stood in the wood-

[ 36 ]

shed with Dad. Even to this day the rays of a setting sun, when I chance to view them through a dusty and cob-webbed window, fill me with a vague uneasiness, and once again that kindly voice is vibrant in my ears.

"Well, son, I suppose you know you have disrupted the natural sequence of things—as usual?"

"Sir?"

"Your mother is on the verge of—well—she insists that I do something. Now let's get at the bottom of this. Where did you get that trout?"

"Just below the dam, sir."

"Oh! A fine pool. Were there any more?"

"No, sir. He—"

"Naturally you wouldn't see them. It is hardly possible he would be there alone. What did he take?"

"A frog, sir."

"A very good bait at times," he said, and then fell silent for a long long moment, while I stood uneasily, shifting restlessly from foot to foot as I awaited the verdict. Then he continued:

"I shall have to punish you, I suppose, but not until we have gone into the matter thoroughly. After this has blown over a bit—say in three or four days—we will go down there some morning and try to reconstruct the scene."

Time marches on—until I am ten, or perhaps eleven. It is not the years, but my stature that counts. I have arrived at that blissful moment for which I have awaited so long. I can, by leaning far back and stretching my arms to the utmost, hoist Old Betsy to my shoulder and crook a finger around the trigger. By the sawhorse and fencerail method I have long since mastered her intricacies, and have learned to take the demoralizing blow which follows each pull of the trigger as inevitably as night follows day. I have killed my first grouse with it, and my second and third, thanks to a convenient limb and the fact that they were all credulous fellows who believed me too small to be taken seriously. We have had several "peep" pies for which I have provided the chief essential in the shape of forty sandpiper breasts. I have played havoc with several sitting flocks of teal, while rails and bitterns, plover and yellowlegs, crows and blue-jays have gone to swell my total and the ranks of the vanquished. Still, I am far from satisfied, for it has been done under the direct supervision of Dad, and all too frequently it has been his supporting hand that steadied the muzzle and caused it to cease its erratic wanderings while I pulled the trigger.

All that is a thing of the past now, for I am about to enter the second phase of my existence. Already the process has begun, for I resent any offer of assistance, and while there is yet no thought in my mind of questioning any parental edict I do think it strange they cannot see I am now old enough to hunt alone. I argue the point with Mother, and suggest it rather diffidently to Dad, but without result other than that in my own deportment. I become at once an exemplary youth, needing only a halo to achieve saintliness, and gradually it has an effect. I am commissioned to go down into the field alone to exterminate a woodchuck, and acquit myself creditably. I am assigned to sentry duty in the corn patch, which a horde of blackbirds is demolishing, and cover myself with glory by downing a basketful of them at one shot. I am sent to rescue a half-grown broiler that a marauding hawk has seized and carried to the edge of the wood, and am fortunate enough to find him so reluctant to leave his easily won meal that I am able to extract the last full measure of revenge.

I sweep the barn from cupola to cellar, clean the henhouse windows, split an enormous amount of kindling, and ask once more. It works! I grab the gun and a handful of shells, rush out of the house and across the fields, and am swallowed up in the woods before anyone has a chance to change his mind. My former caution is thrown to the winds, for I am hunting against time, with six o'clock the absolute deadline, and I go through the woods like a summer cyclone. Grouse whir away before me, or hammer up into trees and look down at me inquisitively. The former are safe for years yet, but the latter are taking unnecessary chances, for although I miss many of them the fates are sometimes kind, and I hurry home while it is yet light, that I may display my prize.

They are glorious days, but there is yet something lacking. The memory of those reports that drifted up from the marshes are still echoing in my ears, and I know I shall never be satisfied until I have spent an evening there alone. I beg the privilege, and am refused, kindly, but in tones which tell me it will be futile to press the point. I try to be satisfied with my lot, but learn that it is the forbidden fruit which tastes the sweetest. I resist the temptation for a time, but a mighty wind roars in from the southeast, and I fall from my pinnacle with a resounding crash.

I ask if I may "go down through the woods," a carefully worded phrase which allays any twinge of conscience I feel at the deception, and when the boon is granted I repair to the house, load myself down with those thirty brass shells, slip the iron "extractor" over my middle finger, shoulder the gun and march in an undeviating line straight "through" the woods and out upon the marshes beyond.

There is yet an hour of daylight, and I hasten it by repairing an old blind by a swale hole where I have previously destroyed several teal. I am still absorbed in my task at sunset, but cease abruptly when a flock of black ducks comes swinging in from the river. I dive for shelter, and pit my strength against that of the mighty hammer spring, but the birds have seen me and sheer abruptly away. I cock the other hammer, twist about so that I may have ample elbow-room, and settle back with a sigh of great content.

Twilight deepens, and through it comes the whispering of wings. I sit stiffly erect and prepare for action. A dozen forms drop down from nowhere and hover over the water, so perfectly bunched that one well-directed shot would take them all, but I wait for them to alight, and the golden opportunity is gone forever, for they suddenly separate, bounce upward into the wind, and disappear as if by magic.

I vow never to make that mistake again, and while I am still muttering my resolve another flock hovers before me exactly as the first one has done, but this time I am sure they are going to alight. I visualize my triumphant return, staggering under the weight of ducks as I offer them in propitiation for my sin, for I am aware of a growing uneasiness within me.

In some vague way I know that I have erred and that a penalty will be imposed, but that anyone will worry about me never once occurs to me. I am comfortable, safe, and entirely happy, and to think that anyone might imagine otherwise is beyond my power of comprehension.

My train of thought is rudely interrupted when, like their predecessors, the ducks wheel as a single unit and vanish into the darkness, while I clench my teeth in grim determination as I await the next flock. They are slow in coming, but I wait with the fortitude that only duck hunters know. It grows light in the east as a moon pushes up above the distant sand dunes and plunges into the last of the storm clouds.

I sit suddenly erect, tense and expectant, for borne to me on the diminishing wind comes the faint honk of geese. It is high overhead, but in a moment or two I sense a change in the sound, as though a discussion had broken out among them. Some sixth sense tells me they have spotted the marshes, and I instinctively know that they are coming down to my pond. I hear them gabbling excitedly as they plane down from the heights, and my heart sets up a wild tattoo within me, but I note with pride that my hand is steady as a rock.

Nearer they come, and nearer. As I slide the gun out a bit more and prepare for action I know that this time there will be no hesitancy and no mistakes. The moment has been foreordained. Its outcome is as inevitable as though it were written in the stars. It is the moment in which I shall justify my existence.

My straining eyes pierce the darkness, and I can see

that long, wavering line swinging sharply down toward me, and filling the night with a wild, weird music. I half raise the gun to my shoulder, for in another moment they will be upon me, when a shrill and well-remembered whistle reaches my ears, and I look about to see a lantern bobbing along at the edge of the marsh.

The geese see it, too, for they bank sharply and disappear with clamorous honkings, but their instinct for self-preservation is not one whit greater than mine. They are more fortunate, though, I think, as I send back an answering call. Then I unload the gun, let the hammers down, and trudge off to meet my fate.

Time drags along on leaden feet, for I am deprived of the gun for a long, long time; but it is mine once more as a reward for such virtue as I have not hitherto attained, and with its winning I am accorded a new freedom. By some miraculous good fortune which I accept but do not try to analyze, the marshes are no longer forbidden territory, and save for a strict rule that I publicly discuss my proposed wanderings, I am free to come and go pretty much as I choose. I swell visibly with my new importance, and, I suppose, become quite insufferable, but it is not to be wondered at. I have emerged from my chrysalis once more. I am now fourteen.

# CHAPTER II

THERE are, I suppose, but few of us who can look back upon the years of our boyhood without feeling a bit of nostalgia. I know it is so in my own experience. The whole period is bathed in a roseate light, and the troubles that vexed me seem unreal and far away.

How different, though, are the adolescent days. I have yet to meet a man worth his salt who can recall them without a feeling of chagrin. All the half-formed ideas that ran riot in his brain during the formative period now begin to crystallize and take shape, and fearful and wonderful indeed is the result. That I escaped with a whole skin was due to unprecedented good fortune, for I defied every known law of ballistics, and learned, as fools do, through experience.

I recall that it was springtime when I saw the last of Old Betsy. I am sure that Dad had contemplated helping me acquire the light Belgian gun on which I had set my heart, but I have a suspicion he entertained some faint hope that the summer's work on the farm would progress equally well if there were no guns on the place for that period. From my viewpoint, the thing was unthinkable, for I considered them the one thing essential to my existence. Had he suggested as an alternative that I get along with one meal a day, I would have accepted it without an instant's hesitation, but the facts of the case were that I was not consulted. Old Betsy disappeared between two days, and the house seemed as vacant as though half the family were gone.

I suppose nothing better can happen to a boy than to be thrown suddenly upon his own resources. For fifty cents I bought a Civil War relic, a muzzle-loading Springfield to which a breech block had been attached, and twenty rounds of .45-70 ammunition. The breech block was a patented affair, modeled after a garden gate, while the gun itself was strongly suggestive of a crowbar; my first shot with it convinced me that it had undoubtedly been used for that purpose on more than one mired cannon, for the bullet's course was as unpredictable as a woman's fancy.

To dispose of it at a profit called for salesmanship of a high order, but I managed it, and in four swaps acquired a lever-action .38-40 Marlin in workable condition. It was fairly accurate, too, but I soon learned the futility of hoping for any more "peep" pies so long as I was confined to shooting single bullets. Misses were all too frequent, and such unfortunates as I did manage to hit were more fitted for sausage meat than anything else; but no great mind was ever baffled for long by so small a problem. I bought a new box of shells, a few pounds of No. 10 shot, climbed on my bicycle and headed for the beach.

[ 46 ]

The plan was primitively simple, although few are fraught with greater danger. Jacking a shell into the chamber, I would stand the gun upright and pour a good-sized handful of shot into the muzzle. Carrying it carefully erect, I would then ride up to a flock of birds, slide down from the saddle, and, with the gun still elevated, bring it to my shoulder. Then I would slap it down on the flock, pull the trigger, and—BOOM! Old Betsy, even in her most cantankerous moods, never handed out anything worse from either end. I did not know that the practice was almost suicidally dangerous, and I doubt if it would have made any difference had I been aware of it, for it certainly raised havoc with the sandpipers. I killed as high as seventeen with one shot, and ten or a dozen were the rule rather than the exception.

Thus the summer passed, and with the coming of fall I acquired the Belgian 12. Oh, what would I not give to know again the thrill that was mine on that glorious day! Compared to the cumbersome 10-gauge, this new creation was lightning fast, and wing shooting at grouse was now a possibility. There was not the slightest doubt in my mind that I could kill every bird that got up within any distance less than a long rifle-shot. Ah, me!

While I had directed quite a bit of lead at flying ducks and geese, I had, until then, been physically unable to get into action on a grouse that had taken wing, and I learned at once to my consternation that the thing was still impossible. The shooting at sitting birds, and the knowledge that I could not possibly handle the heavy gun, had proved to be my undoing. I would steal along through the woods with the hammer cocked and my finger encircling the trigger, vowing by all I held dear to salute the next grouse that so much as fluttered a feather; and then *Whirrrr* one would go, and I would stand there as incapable of movement as a bust of Lincoln. It was a pretty contretemps indeed for one with aspirations like mine, but, try as I would, there seemed to be nothing I could do about it.

I killed grouse, though. Nothing could prevent my doing that, and in their taking I learned much that proved of value to me in later years.

The successful hunter of any game is not necessarily the best marksman, but rather one who thoroughly understands his quarry, and I learned to know grouse in those days as but few of the younger generation will ever have a chance to know them. It seems incredible now that they could ever have existed in such numbers, but exist they most certainly did, and their total has been swelled neither by my youthful imagination nor the passage of years. I have read scientific treatises on grouse, and I have seen it stated that it requires a square mile of cover to provide food for ten birds, but I, for one, know better. Our town was nine miles square, and at least half of it was tilled land or marshes. That left, at best, not more than forty square miles of potential grouse cover. According to the scientist, no more than four hundred birds could exist in that area, yet I knew five market hunters who shot there exclusively each fall, and one of them with whom I was well acquainted told me that he killed more than seven hundred birds in one season, and that the chap with whom he hunted took four hundred more. The other three were good men, if it is permissible to call market hunters that, and it is entirely probable they accounted for as many more. That there were lean years I will admit, but I think the poorest of them were equal to the best we now have.

In any year, though, it was possible to kill a lot of sitting birds, and in those days I had no compunctions whatever. To me, a grouse was a grouse. He and I were engaged in a war in which everything was fair except my attitude toward him. I believed the end justified any means which might be accomplished with a shotgun, and unfortunately for him, it was several years before I changed my mind.

I learned more about the feeding habits of grouse in those early days than I have ever learned since, and I learned it through sheer necessity. While it was true that an occasional grouse fluttered up into a tree, or tried to steal quietly away at my approach, the great majority of them already had a rudimentary education, thanks to the market hunters, and the numbers which coolly sat and invited disaster were far too few to suit my fancy. I spent days on end sitting as motionless as the log which supported me, at the edge of more than one feeding ground, in an effort to find out something of their habits. I pride myself now on the measure of control I exhibited in letting birds go unharmed upon their way in order that I might learn where they were going and why. My observations led me to believe there is nothing about the human figure that will alarm a ruffed grouse as long as the figure is motionless. Hundreds of them have flown directly at me in my days afield, and they sometimes walked so close to me in my youthful experimenting that they were forced to make a detour around my outstretched feet. Not once, so long as I remained still and kept my eyes averted, would they show the slightest trace of alarm; but if I let my gaze encounter that of the beady little eyes which gazed up into my face, that topknot of feathers would snap instantly erect, the bird would say *Cur-rew!* and either steal swiftly and silently away, or make an instantaneous and more tumultuous departure.

Within an hour's tramping distance from my home lay the beginning of a mile-long swamp that was as productive a bit of grouse country as ever lay out-of-doors. On the south and west it was flanked by acre upon acre of old pine growth, so thickly interlaced overhead that no ordinary snow storm would sift through the branches; there was never better winter cover for grouse than old pine. North of the swamp a hardwood ridge rose in a gentle slope that extended for yet another mile; it was spotted throughout its length with thrifty white oak trees which annually bore acorns without number. My laboratory has always been the out-of-doors, but I have never found another like that. In the spring the edge of the pine wood was spotted with nests which held from ten to fourteen eggs each, and as soon as the broods were hatched they moved out into the swamp. All manner of insect and plant life flourished there, and, from early summer until the first hard frosts, berries grew in profusion. It was a grouse paradise, for so thick were the bushes and brier vines that predators, including man, shunned it as though it were a plague, and left the birds to go their unmolested ways. Shooting within that tangle was, of course, impossible, but it was also unnecessary, for when the last of the berries were frost-blackened, the birds came out to forage on the hardwood ridge.

Their journey to the oaks was a rather leisurely affair, for they came straggling along, either singly or in groups of two or three, from a little after sunrise until noon, but their return was accomplished in one-fifth of that time.

While the sun was yet a half-hour high, the first of the lot would come into view, walking unhurriedly, and pausing every few steps to pick at some bit of green leaf or weed seed; but as twilight began to deepen, the pace would quicken, until at the last there were often two or three birds in sight at once. There was no last-minute snatching of tidbits along the way now, but each, with neck outstretched to the limit, hurried down to the safe haven of the swamp. I used to wonder why, with those glorious wings of theirs, the belated ones did not fly in; but although I stayed many a night until dark, I never saw even one resort to that method of locomotion.

Later in the season many of the birds traveled at least a mile to the outlying oak trees whose acorns furnished one of their best-loved foods, but great though the distance was, they walked. Excepting when the ground has been covered with snow and they have been forced to take up their diet of buds, I have never seen them travel to their feeding or roosting grounds in any other manner.

The pines are gone now, and with their passing the swamp has dried out, until today not so much as one flock finds refuge there. I regret it, for it was as sweet a shooting ground as I have ever seen. No amount of hunting could ever clean out all the birds there, but the cutting of their winter cover did it very effectively; and that, I believe, is the major reason why the grouse in my section of New England, at the peak of their periodic increase, fall far short of their old time high.

Many a bird I brought home from the edge of that hardwood ridge, but even then it left a bad taste in my mouth, for more than anything else in the world I wanted to be a wing shot. I could analyze my trouble easily, but correcting it was an entirely different matter; and try as hard as I would for that first year, I could not force myself to shoot at so much as one flying bird. It made no difference if I saw it first, and knew that it was going up: the moment it started I was stricken with a paralysis that held me in a grip of iron until the hurtling form was lost to my view.

To illustrate how serious it was, I remember one occasion when, in crossing an open glade between two jutting points of birch growth, I ran upon a flock of grouse in its very center. The ground was covered knee-deep with grass which effectually concealed them, but there was neither tree nor hindering shrub to interfere with my vision or mar the perfect conditions.

I was well up to them when a bird got up and rose at a steep slant to clear the tops of the bushes thirty yards away. No man's imagination is fertile enough to picture a better opportunity than that, but I stood there, rigidly as though carved from stone, while thirteen grouse got up, one after

[ 53 ]

another, and flew in that same line. Even now, after all the years, it stands out as one of the bitterest moments of my life.

If I were offered the privilege of living my life over again, I think the memory of those days would cause me to refuse. The disappointments were so cruel, the nights so filled with self-recrimination, that what went before or what was to come after, could hardly recompense me for the agony I suffered. Until then the fates had been kind, but now they had either turned their backs upon me, or, as I sometimes fancied, even conspired together to devise some heinous plan further to rack my tortured soul. Well can I recall one such instance.

There was a turkey-fancier in town: an inventive sort of person, who thought, and rightly, too, that a judicious mixture of wild stock among his inbred fowls would increase their stamina. Accordingly he had two toms and a half dozen hens sent up from Kentucky. They were supposed to be three-fourths wild stock, but later events proved it to be a very conservative estimate.

In that sleepy and snowbound town, an event such as this ranked as first-page news, and in the course of a few days the entire population drove in to see them. Quite naturally the birds fascinated me, for they looked not unlike glorified ruffed grouse, and many were the fanciful pictures

I painted of what I would do if I were ever so fortunate as to stumble upon a flock of them in their native habitat. That it was but a fanciful picture I later came to learn.

Save for a telltale look of the wild in their eyes, the flock apparently became entirely domesticated, and with the coming of spring the proud owner deemed the time ripe to let them range with the others. The result was one that he might have foreseen, for with a chorus of happy *Put-puts* the flock scaled the fence and planed off to the woods a quarter mile away.

What followed was natural, I suppose, but I have always regretted it. I wish I might record that they increased and multiplied, but such was not the case. The news spread like wildfire, and the male population rallied to arms like the farmers at Lexington. They surrounded the wood and converged toward the center, penning in the helpless birds and forcing them at last to run the deadly gauntlet. Only one of the ill-fated eight won through unscathed, and he, in the course of a few days, made his way down to the strip of woods that divided our farm from the marshes.

I heard him calling plaintively down there one morning, and I vowed that on the morrow we would have turkey for dinner. No bird his size could invade that domain with impunity, for I knew every inch of the ground and every last thicket which might afford him shelter.

[ 55 ]

I found him without difficulty, for he continuously uttered that lonesome call, but at my approach he ran as only a turkey can run, before I came within range. With all the skill I possessed (and even yet I like to think it considerable), I headed him down the mile-long length of that cover, and drove him out at last upon a jutting point where he could not double back past me without being seen. My heart warmed within me, for our turkey dinner seemed assured.

At the top of the jutting point a tangle of blueberry bushes grew so thickly that they effectually screened him from my prying eyes, but I knew he was there, and I knew, too, that he could not escape me. If I could kill ducks and crows on the wing, any bird the size of this one would be an easy mark. I pushed the gun ahead, bent my finger around the trigger and went confidently on.

It has been said that the boldest course is the safest, but I think my purpose would have been better served had I chosen a program of watchful waiting. Or perhaps the author of the statement had in mind a harried and harassed quarry. The turkey chose a course that was bold enough, for he lay so closely concealed in a patch of bushes that I almost stepped on him. He came out with a raucous and despairing cry and a thunderous roar of wings that dwarfed to insignificance the mightiest effort of any ruffed grouse I had ever encountered, but with an entirely different effect upon me. Instead of standing rigidly as I had habitually done, I jumped backward so violently that I tripped in the brush and fell sprawling; when I scrambled to my feet the turkey was but a speck on the distant horizon, nor have I seen either that one or another of its kind from that day to this.

Had it not been for my inability to kill grouse on the wing, I think I would have been entirely happy, for I had almost unrestricted freedom where shooting was concerned. I was privileged to hunt the marshes and to stay as long as I chose, and it was not long before I chose to stay all night. Procuring a discarded miner's tent and a rusty oil stove, I set out for ducks in grand fashion.

The point of woods where I bade farewell to my turkey jutted well out into the marsh, and intercepted the aerial lane where the ducks used to trade back and forth between the river and the marshes. It was there I pitched my tent, and many a moonlight night I crouched in front of the open flap and saluted flock after flock as they winged past. Then, wrapped in blankets upon my brush cot, I would fall asleep to the accompaniment of their whistling wings, only to awaken at the first crack of dawn that I might intercept them upon their return.

Thus passed my fourteenth autumn and a part of my

fifteenth—and then an event occurred which, in one fleeting moment, changed my whole outlook upon life as completely as anything in the world could have changed it.

One of my youthful acquaintances was an unfortunate chap whose father believed that the one thing a boy should have beside work, was more work. Other fathers have cherished a similar belief, but this one actually practiced it, and drove the youngster to unremitting toil. The sad part of it all was that he always held out as a reward for yet greater endeavor, a mythical day's vacation when the last bit of work was done; but because the youth was the only boy on a tremendously large farm, that golden moment never came.

For several years we had been planning to drive to a neighboring town where a distant relative of his lived, and indulge in a glorious day's hunt. The country, as I afterward learned, was not one whit better than that which bordered our own dooryards, but it had the enchantment which distance always lends; and to add to its attractiveness, the relative had informed him that the woods were not only full of partridge, but the river that bordered the property was also full of ducks.

Those were the years when we believed everything, and we accepted literally the word "full." If a space was filled with anything, there certainly was no room for more; and many were the visions I had of a veritable wonderland, where grouse crowded one another like hens in a restricted yard, and where the branches of the trees sagged beneath their load of roosting birds.

I had, I remember, ample time in which to dream, for one year sped away, and another was almost gone before the day arrived for which we had waited so long. It was late in the fall, and an inch of snow lay on the ground, but that did not deter us. We started before daybreak, in a Concord buggy drawn by a plodding plowhorse, and reached our destination before the sun was an hour high. Strangely enough, the crowded conditions had not forced any grouse out into the open road. We had rather planned on that, and had taken along a gunny sack in which to store the surplus after the rather shallow wagon-box was filled. I recall, too, that I had borrowed a ball of strong cord, for I had a half-formed fancy that our triumphal return would be somewhat enhanced if we had a string of a dozen or more grouse tied to either shaft.

The woods looked inviting, however, and it was not long before we were in them. There were grouse enough, too, despite the bad conditions, but they apparently had no suicidal tendencies, for when the hurrying sun and a lusty blast on the dinner horn announced the hour of noon, we had bagged not so much as one bird.

We ate the lunches we had carried with us, and supplemented them at the table with fried home-cured ham. To this day I cannot help looking upon that good old New England stand-by with respect, for in some vague way I have always felt that it was in a measure responsible for what happened.

The early afternoon had brought us no more success than had the morning; but swinging over to the river, we had driven a truly tremendous flock of black ducks from a bit of fast water that was as yet unfrozen. They escaped unscathed, but as the afternoon wore on, some hope that they might have returned prompted us once more to swing over that way.

My mind, as we neared the river, was occupied with the thought of ducks and what I would do if so much as one of them got up before me. We were within thirty yards of the river when a grouse burst out from a thicket before me, and with neither hesitation nor unseemly haste I threw the gun to my shoulder and killed her as cleanly and as dead as grouse was ever killed in all the wide world.

I cannot describe my emotions. I was overwhelmed by the incredible happening. I was in a transport of delight. In that one brief moment of time I had been lifted from the plebeian path I had trod, and henceforth I was forever destined to walk with the immortals. Even to this day it warms my heart to recall the moment, for while it is possible that some other youth may have duplicated the feat of killing the first flying grouse at which he shot, I have the satisfaction of knowing that never has the record been bettered.

The bird struck upon the newly formed, black ice near the bank, and slid for a distance of twenty feet out toward the open water in the center; but so greatly was I buoyed up by my mighty achievement, that all unmindful of the paper-thinness of the treacherous stuff, I floated out upon it and retrieved the bird. I would have done exactly the same thing if she had been lying upon the very brink of Niagara Falls. Had she been solid gold, and every last feather set with diamonds, I am sure she could have been no more precious to me. To the other grouse around us and to the remaining hour of daylight, I gave no heed. I wanted more than anything else in the world to go home and lay that glorious bird in my father's hand.

So far as shooting was concerned, the incident marked the turning point in my life, for I never again experienced the old paralysis. In fact, from that moment, it always seemed to me that the sudden flushing of a grouse released some sort of spring within me, for I went into action like a jack-in-the-box, and it was years before I could remain sufficiently calm to take any sort of aim at a flushed bird. It was a handicap, for the birds I bagged were few and far between, but I think if I had it all to learn again I would practice the same system. In later years I have hunted with all manner of marksmen, but I have never seen one who consciously "sighted" his gun who could kill grouse in any place where I could not. In the open, on ducks and geese, I have met my master many a time, but in the brush where lead did not have to be considered, no chap who shut one eye and squinted down the barrel could take birds away from me.

I do not know whether it is possible for everyone to learn to shoot thus, but judging from my own experience I think it can be done. I am sure it would be hard to find anyone with less natural ability than I had, or one who was a more backward pupil, yet I did learn after a weary, weary while to will a charge of shot to land in a certain place, and to have it do so with quite pleasing frequency.

Occasionally one meets a fellow who can pick up any-body's shotgun, go out and acquit himself creditably on all kinds of game, but that chap was born with something which most of us lack. The run-of-the-mill fellow has to specialize on one type of shooting until he masters it. An-other sort of shooting will then come easier than the first, but even so he is quite likely to look foolish until he has learned the peculiarities of the flight of his quarry, and has made a mental correction in his timing.

I remember an occasion which illustrates my point. It was during those trying years when I was endeavoring to determine why it was that I could shoot a pretty fair score on ducks and yet missed grouse with heartbreaking regularity. It seemed logical to believe it was largely a matter of the environment in which each was found. If I could have grouse flying across the marshes as ducks flew across them, there was no reason why I could not hit them with equal ease. The reasoning seemed sound, and later it was responsible for the birth of an idea.

A hundred yards out from one tip of the crescent of woods which fringed the marsh, wandered a shallow creek, and an equal distance beyond it a patch of scrubby pine and gnarled alders stood like a lone sentinel on that level expanse of waste land. Grouse were plentiful enough in the wood, and occasionally when forced out to the tip I had seen one scale off across the creek and light in the oasis of pine. If I could only get them to fly back and forth along that route I could kill them with machine-like precision: hence the plan.

Enlisting the services of another youth, I went down and combed the entire length of that crescent of woods. A number of birds cut back behind us or took refuge in trees, but when we reached the end we had a pretty sizable flock before us. Leaving the boy on guard, I circled out in the marsh and took up my station in the bed of the creek, in what I judged would be the line of their flight. The banks afforded partial shelter, and I knew if I remained quiet they would not deviate from their course once they had started. It was as pretty a location as one could expect to find. I was situated on the main highway, and I was prepared to do a wholesale business. I announced to my assistant that I was ready.

The first bird came out of the woods like a bullet, its feathers flattened down by the wind of its flight until it looked no larger than a robin. On it came, rocking from side to side with a cradle-like motion. It passed me within a distance of twenty yards, and I suppose I missed it by as many feet with both barrels. While I was reloading, a pair started out together, flying about two feet apart, and directly at me. I missed them once as they were coming in, and again after they had passed, and the echoing reports had not died on the vagrant breeze before another one was on its way.

Business, I am sure, was never better, but the profits were negligible. If I remember correctly, the boy drove eleven grouse past me and I emptied sixteen shells at them without so much as loosening a single feather. Then, when the last one had safely landed among the scrubby pines, the boy came over, circled the patch and drove them back again—and I emptied the remaining nine from my one box of twenty-five, with exactly similar results.

The situation was embarrassing to say the least, for I had, I fear, painted a rather glowing picture to the youth concerning the things I would do if he drove any grouse across my path. It required a lot of explaining, but I take credit to myself that I did not place the blame on the gun, nor have I ever done so since. Even an old Puritan bell-muzzle would kill grouse consistently at twenty yards, and few of these birds were beyond that distance. The fault was wholly mine, and I grieved about it for months. Not until long after did I know that I was attempting one of the hardest problems a grouse hunter has to face, for the conditions are as different from those he has trained himself to overcome as black is different from white.

Theoretically, of course, all forms of open shooting are the easiest, but I have yet to meet the crack grouse hunter who does not claim the softest shooting to be those birds which hammer up through the brush before him. He has schooled himself on shots of that nature, and every nerve and muscle coördinate to make his swing and timing faultless, yet more than once I have seen a man who was pretty near tops as a brush shot throw his hat down on the ground and walk around it in aimless circles after shooting at a bird that broke across an absolutely clear opening before him.

Let it be said to my credit, though, that I did not repeat my performance on the marshes. The thought of making another such sorry spectacle of myself was undoubtedly a deterring influence, but it was not grouse hunting as I wished to learn it. The dream I had once cherished of becoming the best all-around shot in the world was daily disintegrating into the substance of which dreams are made, but with its passing the desire to be a brush shooter flourished and grew until it became an obsession. That I have never fully realized it does not matter. Hope springs eternal in the human breast, and I am still enough of an optimist to think, with each succeeding fall, that I will at last reach that pinnacle on which I so long ago set my heart.

While those early years were lean ones, and fraught with disappointments which seemed almost tragic, there were nevertheless events which I still remember with a great amount of satisfaction.

My first dog falls into that category. He was a black-and-white water spaniel. The color I can vouch for personally, but the breeding was largely a matter of conjecture on the paternal side. He was, as the breeder informed me, a "grade" and therefore not eligible to registration, but I have never owned a more intelligent animal, or one who made his way so deeply into my heart. His enthusiasm over grouse was at least equal to mine, and he took to the water like a young seal. No dog ever paid greater allegiance to his master than he, for from the moment his jaws closed on his first duck, he was mine and mine alone. From then until he died he was as much a part of me as my shadow. During the summer he slept upon my bed, and in the winter he slept beside me beneath the blankets. I learned early never to close a door between us, especially if it chanced to be an outer one, for if there was an open window in the room he would be outside almost as quickly as I, and if there were only closed ones I had a job of glass-setting on my hands.

I believe it is the inalienable right of every boy to have a dog for his very own, and if he is to hunt with one in later life, the early lessons he learns will be invaluable to him. I like to think that I know something about training a bird dog. I have owned all sorts since that first one, some of them bad and some of them worse, but if any of them have shown improvement under my tutelage, much of the credit belongs to my inseparable chum of the long ago.

I think most boys have an intuitive good judgment with animals, and the one who can retain that fine intimacy until he grows up will never experience much difficulty in training his dogs. I used no system in training my first one, nor have I ever done so since. They can be ground out along certain prescribed lines, as our children are put through the public schools, but the top-notcher must be dealt with as an individual and by a man who loves and understands him.

I knew nothing about dogs when I brought home that pocketful of small puppy, but there was something akin about us, and I learned to know and understand him as but few of us grown-ups know our dogs. Because I was his god, he wished to please me, and I had but to get a thought home to him and he would immediately put it into execution.

He was the smartest retriever I have ever seen, from either land or water, yet the whole process of teaching him to do it did not take five minutes. I would not advise anyone else to try it, for I have never owned another dog I dared risk it on, but it worked on that one as I knew it would, and illustrated the point I am trying to bring out, that the better a man and his dog understand each other, the easier it will be for both.

The pup was seven months old when I took him down to the marshes for the first time. Naturally he was accustomed to a gun, for I doubt if there had been a day since I brought him home, with the exception of Sundays, that he had not smelled powder smoke, but he had neither sighted nor scented game.

It was early September, and I had seen a flock of teal winging their way across the woods. I knew instinctively the pond hole they would choose, so I grabbed the gun, told the pup to follow, and struck off.

The ducks were where I expected them to be. I could hear their soft chatter as I crept up to the bank. It was not much of a sporting proposition, I fear, for I wanted a duck or two for the pup. Peeping through the long grasses, I picked out a pair sitting close together and let them have it. With frightened squawkings and a great beating of wings the others bounced into the air, leaving their two companions fluttering upon the water. The pup was excited. Some age-old instinct of which he had been unaware until the moment, told him that out there in the water before him fluttered the spirits of two vanquished things whose kind a thousand generations of his ancestors had been trained to retrieve. Every nerve and sinew within him quivered in his eagerness to go after them, but the waters were already chilled by the autumn frosts, and the distance, I suppose, looked great to a small pup.

He walked out a few inches, his gaze centered on one bird that beat round and round in aimless circles with its head held beneath the surface, but he had had no previous experience, so he stood there and whined in his eagerness.

I think I executed good judgment then, for I understood my dog better, I fear, than I have ever understood one since. I knew that I, too, would hesitate before taking that chill plunge, but I knew from past experience that if I had once taken it I would go out and get my birds, and I knew the pup would do the same thing. I picked him up in my arms, waded out to my boot-tops, pointed him toward the ducks and gave him a mighty heave toward them.

He struck with a resounding splash that carried him beneath the surface, but when he came to the top he was headed in the right direction. I can see him now as he reared up, shook the water from his eyes and looked about. The shore was invitingly near, but the ducks were out there before him and he went after them like an old campaigner. With instinctive good judgment he disregarded the one that had ceased its flutterings, and bore down upon the other. Darting his head in beneath the beating wings, he seized the bird by the body, came out and laid it at my feet.

I think now, after all the years, that I have never known a happier moment, for no matter how keen a sportsman one may be, he has missed a great deal if he has never known the intimate companionship of a good dog. I told him how delighted I was, and he understood me. He told me that he was more than a little pleased with himself, and very, very happy. It was all quite foolish, I suppose, and will undoubtedly look doubly so to the man who regards his dog with no more sentiment than he accords his guns, but I still cherish it as one of the big moments of my life.

When we had exchanged our mutual felicitations, I pointed out the other duck to him, and told him to go get it. He went in promptly and brought it out—and the whole business of teaching him to retrieve was accomplished as easily as that. From that moment on, there never was a time when he would not bring in any species of game from land or water; in fact, on the way home that afternoon we came unexpectedly upon the rest of the flock huddled up near a bank at the edge of the creek. They got up before I saw them, but I managed to bring one down with each barrel, and as the last one was falling I heard a splash, and looking down, I saw the pup already in the water, making his way out toward the first bird.

Oh, a fine pair of irresponsible youths we were, but he grew old before his time. I suppose it was my fault, for I hunted with him in all kinds of weather. The *mésalliance* responsible for his birth had robbed him of the protective, spaniel undercoat which should have been his heritage, but it gave him a lion's heart. He would go into the icy brine of midwinter creeks as unhesitatingly as though it were summer, but it took its toll from his unprotected body and robbed me of him all too soon.

While the memory of his first retrieving still stands out so strongly in my mind, the recollection of his last is equally fresh.

It was a blustering March day, with a raw easterly wind which I knew would send all the ducks scurrying for the

[ 71 ]

shelter of the creeks which the strong tides of the ocean kept open, and it called me with an urge that was irresistible.

Some faint glimmer of reason warned me that I should leave the dog at home, but I could not resist the pleading look in his eyes, and I let him come. We beat our way down across the ice-covered marshes, and came at last to a creek. Ducks were trading back and forth between the patches of open water, or coming in, belatedly, from the storm-tossed ocean.

We crept into a niche in the bank, crouched low and waited. My heart was set on nothing less than a pair of blacks; but when a flock of sheldrakes hove in sight, just clearing the surface of the water, and, with the wind behind them, driving up the river like bullets, I could not resist the temptation, and cut down a fat drake. From an epicurean's viewpoint, the bird was worth less than nothing, and I would have held the dog on shore, but he was in the water before I was sure whether or not my shot had connected.

With both wind and tide in his favor, he went out easily, but coming back burdened with the duck was a far different matter. The tide was running out like a millrace, the wind had kicked up a nasty little chop which showed white at the crests, but more perilous than all, the river was studded with great ice cakes which had been loosened by the flood tide and were hurrying down to the sea.

I knew instinctively, before he had fought that tide for half a minute, that he couldn't make it. The wave crests curled into his mouth, and the force of the current was so great that he lost rather than gained distance. Then an ice cake weighing tons bore relentlessly down upon him.

He saw it when it was too late, and tried frantically to win past its edge, but it caught him and bore him down. He came up from behind it a moment later, coughing weakly, but still holding the duck tightly clasped in his jaws. Then a wave broke fairly upon him and he went down once more.

I think I have never since been in such a mental state, for so great was the turmoil within me that I could think neither clearly nor sanely. I must have had some wild impulse to go out there after him, for when a glimmer of reason did return I had one hip boot off and was struggling with the other.

The dog came up again, fighting weakly, and then did a thing as indicative of a well defined reasoning power as anything I have ever seen an animal do. Twisting the duck around, he thrust it under him so that its buoyant body kept his nose above water, and then relaxed and lay there limply, resting. With one boot-top flopping around my foot, and the other lying forgotten in the mud, I ran down the bank until I was well below him, and called to him. He had both

[ 73 ]

wind and tide to aid him then, and foot by foot he made his way toward shore, while I waded out at the last until the water was up to my armpits and caught him as he was sweeping past.

He was too far spent to walk, so I wrapped him in my coat and carried him home, hugging him to me and crying because he lay so lifelessly in my arms.

I look back upon our years of companionship with a great happiness, and yet with a great regret. I doubt if such a pair of vagabonds as we ever before roamed those marshes. I know that none were ever happier, but I wish I had been a bit more prudent, at least where winter hunting was concerned. Had I done so it is possible I might have kept my pal for another year or two, for he did not rally as he should, but lay listlessly by the kitchen stove, and grew weaker with each passing day.

It was a languorous, April day when I buried him, at the head of the southern slope below the orchard, with a blanket about him, and his head pointed toward the marshes he had loved so well. They have never seemed the same to me since. The loons still cry lonesomely from the rivers, and the gulls wheel past on effortless wings. Each spring and fall the faint, far honking of geese comes eerily down from the heights. Ducks wheel and circle around the pond holes, and all nature calls as it used to call in those lost, never-again days. Sometimes when the old hurt comes back to my heart, I steal down through the orchard and whisper to him again the words I whispered so often in those other days:

"Come on, boy. Let's go."

I wait there a moment, but the words have lost their magic, and he does not stir in his dreamless sleep. Then, as I stand there, with the old, tight ache in my throat, I think that if in handling other dogs I have owned, I have tempered justice with mercy, and have tried to win them by love rather than force, the virtue, if virtue it be, can quite justly be attributed to the little, black-and-white spaniel who lies in the unmarked grave which everyone but me has forgotten.

I have pondered often about the mental reactions of other youths, and have wondered if I were any different than they. Do they enjoy their glamorous, golden days as I enjoyed mine, and are their disappointments as hard to bear? I know that during those first shooting seasons I lived in an exalted realm far above the prosaic world in which ordinary mortals moved. To cradle a gun under my arm and strike off to roam the woods and marshes was my dream of paradise, but yet I was weighted down with a secret sorrow that was almost more than I could bear. I was, or so I fancied at least, the poorest wing shot in the whole world.

Looking back at it now, I imagine I was as good as other youths of my age, but I had the unhappy faculty of forgetting the hits I scored, while the misses lived on in my memory until they haunted my dreams at night.

Since that memorable day when I had killed my first flying grouse, I had schooled myself to shoot at any bird which rose within range if I could see so much as a disturbance of the leaves to mark the course of its flight. Naturally, I occasionally pulled off a shot so flawlessly perfect that Annie Oakley might have envied me, but it never compensated for the misses I made; and as the latter were far more numerous than the hits, I lived in a state of perpetual torment. Some queer mental twist has always made me attribute any phenomenal shot I have made to pure and unadulterated good luck, yet it will not permit me to console myself with the thought that a miss is but the ill fortune one must learn to expect to find mixed in with the other kind. I have killed scores of grouse from inconceivably difficult positions; but if I were to concentrate for hours on the task I could not recall them all, yet it seems as though all the errors I have ever made stand out glaringly in the spotlight of my memory.

Once, while drinking from a little brook, a grouse flushed from the opposite bank before me. Lying flat on my stomach I reached with one hand for the gun which lay beside me, raised myself up a few inches with the other, and killed the bird cleanly. On several different occasions I have bagged grouse while I was in the act of falling. Tripping, and pitching forward in that step necessary to establish a firm shooting position, as the bird went up, I have thrust the gun forward with one hand even while I was going down, and placed the charge of shot where I had willed it to land; but I recall the occasions with difficulty and with not the slightest sense of pride. They seemed to me to be merely the breaks of the game which I had the right to expect.

How different, though, were those all-too-frequent times when I muffed an opportunity which any duffer should have taken with his eyes shut. There was no laying that at the door of the fickle goddess. The element of luck did not enter into the matter at all. The whole sum and substance of it was that I was a rotten marksman, had always been, and would always continue to be. Day after day, for many a weary year, I made those disheartening misses, and nothing within my power could prevent me from doing so. Many were the tears of shame I shed in those formative days; I could fill a book with accounts of those mistakes, for even yet they occupy a place in my mind which should be filled with happy memories. I still blush at the recollection of one such happening. It was a cruel lesson, but it taught me something which I have never since forgotten whenever a flock of birds suddenly looms before me.

Geese were migrating. For two days a sleety rain had fallen, and many low-flying flocks had winged their way across the marshes. From morning until night since the storm had started, I had haunted that level expanse, but without avail. Always I seemed to be in the wrong place, yet if I moved, as I often did, the position I had so recently vacated became the one spot in all that area over which they would fly. It was particularly discouraging, and doubly so because of the fact that I had yet to kill my first goose; for since that moment when my father's whistle had robbed me of a golden opportunity, some perverse fate had dogged my footsteps where geese were concerned.

By late afternoon of the second day the sleet stopped falling and the storm clouds lifted, but as the skies lightened, my heart grew heavier, for my chance of securing the prize I so much coveted grew less with each passing minute. Doggedly determined, though, not to give up until the last moment, I repaired to the river just as dusk was falling, and crouched in a hole in the bank before a favored eelgrass bed.

I had been there scarcely ten minutes before a fine flock of black ducks came winging up the river to circle close above me. The temptation was great, but my heart was set on nothing less than a fine old gander, and I let them go unmolested upon their way.

As though it were a reward for the self-control I had exhibited, there came to my ears almost instantly thereafter the faint honking of geese, following along the ocean's shore line from the east. Nearer they came, until they reached the mouth of the river. It was a tense moment. Would the smell of fresh water turn them, or would they continue along on their course? Then, all at once, I could detect a new note in their cries, a sort of discordant babbling, as though they were taking a vote on the question.

In my forty years of hunting I have done quite a bit of waterfowl shooting, in various places and under varying conditions, but I have yet to find anything connected with the sport that is more thrilling than those hushed moments of waiting for a wise old gander to make his decision. It far exceeds any thrill I ever got from the actual shooting.

It seemed to me, shivering with cold and excitement as I waited there, that they would never come to an agreement, but all at once the discord ceased, a satisfied and not unmusical honking took its place, and my heart leaped anew as I realized they were coming toward me.

They were as yet a quarter of a mile away, and I had ample time in which to plan my attack. The river at that point was perhaps sixty yards in width, and there was a possibility that they might come in along the opposite shore, but I was prepared for just such an emergency. In each barrel of the double gun I carried, a heavy load of No. 2's rested. I broke the gun, drew the shell from the left barrel, slipped another loaded with BB's in its place, pushed the safety up and twisted around into shooting position. At any distance from one to sixty yards I was ready for them.

Their cries grew louder, and presently my straining eyes picked them up in the gathering darkness, a hundred yards away, and fifty or more feet high, but planing down in a long slant that would terminate slightly on my side of the center of the river and almost exactly before me. After years of futile crawling through mud and slime, and fruitless waiting and freezing in water-soaked holes such as I now occupied, my big moment had at last arrived.

Even yet, after all the years, I cannot help feeling a bit of respect for the hot-headed, impetuous youth who waited there in the shadows of the cut bank. Scores of times since then I have crouched in duck and goose blinds, or waited beside game trails, and tried to still the pounding of my heart because I firmly believed it was hammering loudly enough to alarm my quarry, yet when at last I brought the gun to my shoulder it would cuddle there as steadily as though we were both cast in bronze.

I reacted no differently on this occasion. Nearer the

flock came, dropping easily down, and swinging in a bit more closely toward me. Then just as the leader came abreast of me, he banked sharply upward to check speed, while eighteen others, back-pedaling mightily with their broad pinions, slid tightly in around him and settled slowly down toward the water. Scarcely thirty yards away, and so closely bunched that they seemed like one solid mass, it presented such an opportunity as I had not pictured even in my fondest dreams. With hands grown suddenly steady, I leveled the gun upon the exact center of the flock, looked down the length of the barrels to be sure I was right—and pulled both triggers almost simultaneously.

"WHAM—BAM!" If Lloyd's of London had offered for the small sum of a dime to guarantee me at least six geese from that flock I would not have paid the premium. It was unimaginable that two-and-one-half ounces of shot could find its way through that congestion without taking heavy toll, but to the best of my knowledge and belief they ruffled not so much as a single feather. With startled cries the flock milled about, and then climbed rapidly upward with a tremendous roar of beating wings. I had ample time in which to slip in two more shells and drive the charges upward among them but I did not do it. Instead, I climbed from the hole, stuck the gun under my arm without even bothering to extract the empty cases, and struck off home-

[ 81 ]

ward, vowing by everything I held sacred that never again so long as I lived would I bestow on any firearm so much as one disdainful glance. I mooned over my disappointment for days, but gradually I evolved a moral from the heart-breaking experience, and I have adhered rigidly to it ever since. If I were to be privileged tomorrow to shoot into a flock of a hundred geese, packed three deep in a ten-foot area, I would pick one lone bird, make sure of him, and let happy chance take care of any shot which went astray.

I do not know how I would have survived those painful years had it not been that I extracted one small gleam of comfort from the fact that I was improving in my shooting at grouse. The improvement was an infinitesimal one, and its progress could not be gauged by weeks or months, but with each passing year my score went up a few points, and I found myself occasionally connecting with chances which would hitherto have been impossible. It was a slow and discouraging process, and I suppose that is why success seemed so desirable, and has remained so distinctly worth-while after I had achieved some small measure of it. In my later years I have looked over a gun barrel at almost every species of New England game, with the exception of moose, but I have never had a day that I would not gladly exchange for another like any one of hundreds I have spent shooting grouse. No other bird I know begins to compare

LYNN
BOGUE
HUNT

with him in the infinite variety of difficult targets he presents. No other game bird is possessed of such an assortment
of tricks, and no other can so safely guarantee that despite
the rapidly changing conditions in which the automobile
has played so prominent a part, he will continue to perpetuate his species with little or no help from mankind.

Ducks and geese, and all manner of shore birds and
four-footed creatures had played their part in those youthful years while I was finding myself, but gradually they
were relegated to their rightful second place and grouse
became ever more important in my scheme of things. I had
developed a fondness for going down into that Maine
country I had learned to love in childhood, for a week or
two with the white-tails, but it was not long before I was
delaying the trips until the grouse season had ended; and
with the change in laws which made that no longer possible, I gave it up entirely. It was a good sport and I loved
it, but I could not afford to pay the price of those days I
must sacrifice from my favorite coverts.

For two dollars I bought a black-and-white setter pup
(also ineligible for registration) and brought him home as
soon as his eyes were open. I reared him on a bottle, and
watched him grow into the strangest-appearing setter on
which man ever looked. No one sire, I am sure, was ever
responsible for all those varying characteristics, for his head

[ 83 ]

was that of an English bulldog, his coat pure Airedale in color and texture. He had the body of a foxhound, and the tail of a rat terrier, but he also possessed a setter's nose, and a disposition toward humans that was angelic. Without benefit of book learning, kindly advice or previous experience, I taught him to stand grouse more staunchly than many of the bluest of bluebloods, and with that not inconsiderable feat to my credit we began to take birds with some measure of consistency.

No dog over which I have ever hunted could give me a more interesting day, for the human race was the only species of live thing he would tolerate. Any four-footed creature that could climb a tree did so immediately when he put in his tumultuous appearance, and those that couldn't climb, tried mightily to, and perished in their trying. He had the most violent antipathy toward skunks that one could imagine, and found them in all sorts of unsuspected places. He seemed to think no day complete until he had demolished at least one of them, and he went about it with a reckless abandon that was heart-warming.

This was always interesting to watch, but it had its drawbacks, for he always came in immediately afterward and either jumped upon me in his exuberance, or else inadvertently rubbed against me so that I too became a social pariah. I have always fancied, though, that the aroma which preceded us through the woods worked to our advantage, for all manner of game stood calmly while we approached, and stared curiously at us; and even grouse in coverts which were hunted the hardest would twitter nervously and either hop up on a low branch or move quietly aside in the simple belief that we were no more dangerous than we smelled.

Growing accustomed to each other in our three years of close harmony, we were getting to be quite a deadly combination, when the dog made the fatal mistake of thinking he could disconcert a fast express train by running beneath one of the coaches and barking at the other side. He had done it repeatedly with freights and locals, but the seventy-mile pace was faster than his calculations, and I was once more without a dog.

Such a condition was unthinkable, but another change was taking place within me. If such a thing were humanly possible, I was even more enthusiastic about grouse hunting than ever, but I was beginning to feel that their taking would be greatly enhanced if I owned a thoroughbred setter. That, at least, was what I told myself, and I suppose I believed it implicitly then, but now I strongly suspect the real reason was of a slightly different nature. I had a mental picture of the only dog that would satisfy me, a silky-haired, snow-white specimen of such ethereal beauty that ladies, especially if they were young and good-looking, would stop and gasp in admiration at the sheer beauty of us both.

I had arrived at that perilous age when I spent an inordinate amount of time before the mirror, parting my heavily pomaded hair in its geometrical center, wearing collars over which I peered with difficulty, and showing a marked preference for widely-flaring, peg-top trousers with violent checks. The cocoon in which I had been encased was splitting under the strain, and when I emerged from it at last I soared to a newer and more glorious height. I was twenty-one years old.

# CHAPTER III

IF there is anywhere a man who loves guns better than I, we have never met. There is a psychological reason for it, I suppose, and I think it is because they were so hard to acquire in my youth—and still are, for that matter. I knew every gunsmith and gun dealer within a day's drive before I was fifteen years old, and I suppose they knew me much better, for I must have been something of a problem to them.

I had one advantage over them, though, for while I was always acutely aware of the state of my finances, it was of necessity a matter of conjecture on their part, and although I have no doubt they all shrewdly estimated the trifling nature of my resources, I was still a potential customer, and they could not well refuse to show me their one stock in which I was interested.

While barter is the oldest system of trade, it was the Yankee who elevated it to an immortal plane, and on one side of the house at least, my ancestors had been New England bred for two hundred years. There is a finesse about the art which the uninitiated will never know. No true Down-Easter versed in the finer tricks of the trade ever asked the question, "How will you swap?" That would have put him on the defensive at once. It was his way first to create a demand for his product, and then let the other fellow ask the question. I figured that out, unassisted, as far back as the time when I owned the old Springfield. When the outgoing tide had bared the goose rocks off our beach, it was not an uncommon sight to see a dozen or more seals basking in the sunlight upon them. Whether or not the State was still paying the oldtime fifty-cent bounty upon them I do not remember, but I recall that my campaign was based upon that assumption. I could not play it from a sporting angle, but I did paint a rather rosy picture of the financial independence that would be mine when I collected a half dollar bounty for each of the nineteen shells that remained of my original twenty. That I was careful to paint it verbally, in the presence of several youths of my own age, was a credit to my sagacity, and when I detected a gleam of avarice in the eyes of one of the lot I directed my talents on him alone.

It was he who made the advances and it was I who held back, only to capitulate reluctantly at the last. From my original investment of fifty cents, I acquired a Stevens' Favorite .22, which functioned after a fashion, a pair of skates, a musical top, a glass aggie, two brass harness buckles and other articles too numerous to mention.

Thus began as interesting an avocation as I have ever known, and from which I learned not only something concerning firearms, but human nature as well. I did not always fare so well as in that first venture, for the fascination which guns held for me often proved to be my undoing. It was inevitable that I should meet some who were as unscrupulous as I, and some who were far more shrewd, but I did manage in a few years to own briefly a varied assortment of guns, and to acquire a certain amount of knowledge concerning them.

I believe it was about the time when I reached man's estate that I ordered my first custom-built gun. While it was a fact that I was killing grouse then, I was far from being the Dead-eye Dick I had expected to become, and the human equation had entered into my calculations. I knew the fault was largely mine, that my misses were not the results of a defective pattern but of my holding, and I labored under the belief that it was possible to build a gun so fitted to my physical characteristics that it would point itself automatically.

Through the trial-and-error method I had evolved a fanciful gun which I firmly believed would solve all my problems. In those days I was thin as a re-sawed lath and stood almost six feet in height, and, shooting as I did with both eyes open, I found it hard to draw my neck in enough to bring the breech at all near my line of vision. With a worthless old double-gun as a base for my experiments I spent days in remodeling it into a try-gun with an adjustable stock, and worked out a formula I thought perfect.

My order, as I remember it, specified a 16-gauge double-gun, with Damascus barrels, to weigh as near six-and-one-quarter pounds as it was possible to make it. I specified an extra-thick breech, with the barrels tapering to a thinness to be determined only by the factor of safety, my idea being to have the weight concentrated in the center so that alignment of the tubes would be lightning fast. As a further proof of my poor judgment, I ordered twenty-five-inch barrels and a stock with a three-and-one-half-inch drop.

Enclosing the required deposit, I mailed my letter, and settled back to wait, with what fortitude I possessed, through the six long weeks which must elapse before I should see my brain-child. I was buoyed up by one thing, though, for I had formed a mental picture of the surprise and delight of the gun-company officials when they received my order. I could see the white-haired old president calling a meeting of the board of directors, and addressing them in some such manner as this:

"Gentlemen, we have something here! A gun that will revolutionize wing shooting! Our fortunes are made, and we owe it all to that genius down in Maine who has discovered a principle which our engineers have so long overlooked."

Consequently, I was more than a trifle surprised when, a few days later, I received a letter from them, stating that because the specifications were so unusual, and the finished product would be so impractical and unsalable in the event I did not accept it, they would require the full amount of the order in advance.

I sent them a long-distance look of disdain, a contemptuous snap of the fingers—and the money.

The gun arrived in due course of time. I unwrapped it, swabbed out the grease, and snapped it together. It was fast, all right. Its speed and ease of handling exceeded my expectations, but its feather-lightness about the muzzle seemed a bit unusual. It felt, to put it mildly, as unstable as a feather in a stiff breeze, but I excused that on the grounds of my unfamiliarity with such a supreme bit of artistry, and took it out behind the barn to test its shot pattern.

I had specified a cylinder bore in the right barrel and a full choke in the left, and they performed beautifully. The cylinder opened up nicely with a well distributed pattern at twenty-five yards, and the choke smacked them smartly home at forty. It had been years since I had recalled that a gun had a recoil, but now I was reminded of it sharply, for it not only awakened memories of Old Betsy, but was also suggestive of an army mule.

In my ignorance, I attributed it to the make of the gun

rather than the abnormal drop, and looked about for something wearing feathers on which to try it further. It was an overcast day in early September, and even as I stood there I saw a flock of half a dozen ducks swing up from the marshes and head upriver. I knew their destination: a sheltered pool at the head of a long, broiling run that foamed along for two or three hundred yards between jagged, upthrust boulders. On either bank a thick growth of brush made a quiet approach to the pool an impossibility, but more than once I had taken ducks there by wading the stream where it was shallow, and jumping from rock to rock in the deeper portions. Pulling on a pair of hip boots, I grabbed another handful of shells and started out.

The river, I found when I reached it, was higher than usual, for many of the lesser rocks were submerged, while around the larger ones the waters creamed and foamed like a millrace. It was precarious traveling, but I was never one to balk at obstacles of that nature, and I kept resolutely on. At last I neared the end of the run. Twenty-five yards beyond, the river bent at an abrupt angle which hid the pool from my sight. Listening intently, I could hear above the roar of the waters the soft gabbling of ducks and I knew that in another minute I would have an opportunity to prove the worth of the weapon. But almost at the beginning of the bend I encountered a new difficulty. Most of the stepping stones I had previously used were now covered by the hurrying flood, and only the taller ones remained exposed. Until then these had been close enough together to make progress fairly easy, but now I found myself standing on a flat slab of stone whose surface was just awash, with the next possible foothold six feet upstream, rising some two feet higher than the rock on which I was standing, and presenting a wet and glassy side that slanted upward at a forty-five degree angle. The jump was something to test the powers of an athlete, for it was an uphill affair and had to be accomplished practically square-footed. I could sense that merely to reach the rock would not be enough. I would have to strike it at least halfway up, holding the gun aloft in one hand, in order that my other hand might be free to reach down and secure a steadying grip at the apex of that slippery triangle.

Mentally estimating the drag of those four-pound boots, I gathered myself and leaped. My feet struck where I had willed them to, and my left hand shot down to grasp the rock, but in that instant while I hung there poised, off balance, those cursed boots shot out from under me as though I were standing on wet glass, and I went down heavily. I can feel again in fancy the numbing pain as my right elbow smashed against the rock, directly, of course, upon the protruding "funny bone." Before my horror-struck eyes I saw my fingers uncurl lifelessly from the grip, while as deliberately as though it were being shown in slow motion, the gun on which I had set my heart turned in the air, crashed down upon the rock, slid forward and disappeared, muzzle first, into the hurrying flood.

I have carried all manner of guns, under all manner of conditions and in all manner of places for forty years. With them tucked under my arm or held more carefully aloft I have fallen thousands of times, but never before or since has another one of them slipped from my grasp. There are not many, I fear, who can understand how I felt as I lay there across the rock and gazed down into the hurrying waters. By the sweat of my brow I had earned the money the gun had cost, but I am sure that phase of it never entered my mind. No one has a greater contempt than I for the cheap, mail-order monstrosities which flood the country, but no heathen ever looked upon a carved idol with greater reverence than I bestow upon a good gun, no matter what may be its age or bore or maker. I have never seen one that I did not love and wish that I might own, and I would that my arsenal comprised a hundred of them rather than its meager two or three.

Down there beneath me, in the yellow waters, I momentarily caught the outline of the unfortunate weapon. It was standing upon its muzzle, and the Circassian walnut stock rested securely against the boulder on which I lay. The butt plate was three feet below the surface, but I went down after it, head first, with one arm extended and my legs gripping the rock.

The gun, when I drew it up and drained the water from it was, even to put it mildly, a mess. Upon the polished stock that abominable boulder had stamped a four inch scar which neither time nor rubbing could ever heal. Halfway down the right barrel appeared a dent in which one could almost lay a teaspoon, while the muzzle of the same tube was so flattened against the other that the aperture was not more than a quarter of an inch wide. Many, many times in those weary years that had gone before, I had come back from a day afield in an unenviable frame of mind, but no homecoming in my experience had been so sad as this.

If ever a gun needed to be returned to the factory for repairs, that one did, but my financial resources had been taxed to the limit to acquire it in the first place, and an added bill would force me into bankruptcy. Then, too, the shooting season was only a matter of two weeks away, and it was highly improbable that the gun would be returned to me in less than a month. I decided to test my own resourcefulness.

My first thought was, that because of the extreme thinness of the barrels, the dents might be successfully shot out.

I was aware there was an element of danger in it, but I thought, and rightly, there was opening enough in the muzzle to make it safe. Accordingly I slipped in a shell, closed my eyes, twisted my head away and pulled the trigger, but the result was not up to my expectations, for the opening was not enlarged by so much as a hair's breadth. I tried it again and again, with no better luck, but I did make an interesting discovery. That flattened barrel would spread a charge of shot out into a narrow band that opened up, at thirty yards, into a well-nigh perfect pattern about one foot wide and four feet long, and it would do so with a consistency that was amazing. I thought seriously of hammering the other tube down in an opposite direction and using one barrel on straight-away or rising birds, and the other on cross shots. I still believe there are possibilities in the idea, and wish mightily I could have tried it out on that flock of geese; but I spent hours in filing a steel rod down to a force fit in the cylinder barrel, then polished it with emery cloth, greased it well and drove it through. It was a crude method, but so perfectly did it work, that although a number of hunters handled the weapon in the few months I continued to own it, not one of them ever noticed a mark on it, other than the ineradicable scar upon the stock.

I learned a number of things from that gun in the next month, and not only lost the contempt I had felt concerning the judgment of the men who made it, but much of my egotism as well. The extreme lightness at the end of the barrels was a great mistake. There was no question that the weapon was lightning fast, but it had no more steadiness than a buggy whip. I do not mean that the gun itself was not rigid enough, but there was no muzzle weight to steady the swing or to carry it along when once it was started. It was jerky rather than smooth, and one had to grip the fore end and swing his whole body rigidly on a cross shot, instead of letting the inertia of the gun do the work. I detest any gun that is muzzle-heavy, but I'll take it every time in preference to one that is too light.

The extra drop in the stock was also a mistake. It was true that it brought the sighting plane nearer the eye level which I thought I must forever maintain, but if it was any advantage I paid for it dearly in another respect. Old Betsy had had a pile-driving wallop that had pushed and shoved me around disgracefully, but this thing struck at me with all the speed and venom of a rattlesnake.

I recall an early experience with it which was far from pleasing. There was a bunch of woodcock in a nearby cover, and thither I went to see if I could solve the intricate problem of mastering the peculiarities of my problem child.

Birds were abundant, the afternoon was warm, and it was not long before my clothing was soaked with perspiration. The temperature dropped sharply as the sun went down, and my clothing was like ice upon me as I started for home; but I wondered, as I hurried along, why my right side should remain so stickily warm, while all the rest of my body was tingling with cold. Becoming more curious, I at last unbuttoned my shirt and found that that little spitfire of a gun had hammered a seam of my hunting coat so far into my shoulder that blood was running down to the waistband of my trousers.

I didn't like it, frankly, but there was nothing I could do about it that fall but grit my teeth and take it, and, incidentally, to plan what my next one would be like. I was quite firmly convinced of one thing. This little gun was the fastest thing to handle that I had ever seen, but I would gladly sacrifice some of its excess speed for a bit of stability. I still fancied the drop of the stock was correct, for I had yet to learn about pitch and comb dimensions, and I quite foolishly fancied the excessive recoil was a characteristic of that particular make of weapon. Alas, how much we know when we are twenty-one!

Notwithstanding its inauspicious beginning, that season was an outstanding one in my life, for several things happened which were without precedent in my experience. Most important of all, I killed more grouse than I had taken in any previous year. It was encouraging, for I was well aware that I was handicapped by the gun, and also it was a year when the birds were not up to their high peak. My shooting was definitely improving. For several years I had been keeping tally of the grouse I killed on the wing, by cutting a notch in a stick which I carried in a pocket of my gunning coat. It was a crude system, inspired, I believe by Robinson Crusoe's method of keeping his calendar, but it was simple, and certainly no one ever devised a less cumbersome way of keeping books. Although the number of notches had increased each year, my tally stick had always been so short that I was troubled at times to locate it; but this fall the season was not half over before I found it necessary to transfer the score to a longer bit of wood, and when the battle ended, there were sixty-four indentations upon it. The previous year's record had been my all time high, but this year I had exactly doubled it. At last I could begin to see a ray of hope.

Because I recall using that gun upon them, I remember that it was in late October of that year when I found a flight of strange birds upon the marshes. I had never seen them before, nor have I seen one since, and have never been able to identify them, for the shooting was far too good to spoil by advertising it among any of the local hunters, who might have told me what they were. Unquestionably, they belonged to the tribe of plovers, but they were differently built than any others of their clan. Their plumage was of that typical black-and-white which characterizes the waders, but their lines were almost exactly like those of a quail. The fact that I found them in the long, salt grasses at the extreme upper edge of the marsh, and their short, chunky legs and heavy feet were proof they were not waders. Their bills were only slightly more elongated than those of strictly upland birds, and their wings were so short they seemed wholly inadequate to lift their short, plump bodies from the ground. Although they had the appearance of being somewhat smaller, their weight, I think, was slightly in excess of that of Wilson snipe, but their flight was like that of an arrow released from a bow.

They lay remarkably well, rising frequently at a distance of less than ten feet, and coming up through the grass with a thunder of wings like a young grouse. Then they would level off, just above the tops of the grasses, fly like bullets for thirty or forty yards, then set their stubby wings and plane along for an equal distance before they dropped to earth once more.

I have never seen another bird whose flight was so truly representative of that of the ruffed grouse, nor one that ever helped my shooting more in so brief a time, for it was on them that I learned to curb my impetuous haste. There was (and still is for that matter) something about the sudden thunder of a rising grouse that seems to release a hidden spring within me, and I still find it necessary at times to resist an impulse to blaze away blindly at them before their feet have much more than left the ground. The very fact that one can do so is proof enough there is no need for it, but I have blown to atoms many a bird that I might easily have let get out where the shot would have opened up into a less destructive pattern.

Down there on the marshes, however, with those speckled strangers which were not so highly prized, reason had an opportunity to assert itself. To empty both barrels at one of these fast-flying targets, then to lower the gun and to discover that the little fellow was still not more than thirty feet away, was enough to make even one as dull as I realize that it would be not only more economical, but also more productive, to curb my impetuous haste.

Whether the birds moved on in their migration, or whether I succeeded in bagging them all, I never knew; but before the day came when I was no longer able to find one, I had learned more about shooting than all my previous years had taught me.

It is hard to define the change, for it was so slight that no casual observer would have noticed it, and years were yet to pass before it became instinctive with me, but at last I had blundered into the right path. It is strange how many of us go through life with our eyes closed, and stranger still how blind we are to our own imperfections. No man would take up golf seriously without first consulting a pro, and learning some of the fundamentals of stance and swing and timing, yet the majority of casual shooters never give a thought to these all-important things, and blame their ill luck on a perverse fate that caused them to be born poor marksmen.

There are some so unfortunate as to have defective vision or other physical handicaps, but I believe any normal being can learn to shoot a very creditable score on any species of game if he learns his weakness and conscientiously tries to overcome it.

Watch a squad of good trapshooters at their work of pounding the clay discs into powder, and you cannot fail to notice a great similarity about them. Physically, they may be as unlike as one can imagine, and each will undoubtedly have a style that is distinctly his own, but a careful analysis will disclose the fact that each man's swing, as he goes after his bird, is patterned pretty closely after that of the fellow beside him. I don't know how to describe it, for it is fast without being hurried, and deliberate without being slow. One man may break his birds yards closer than his neighbor, but only because his movements are naturally quicker. I have seen shooters who could almost literally smash their targets off the top of the trap house, and I have seen wing shots make unbelievably quick hits on game when the occasion demanded it, but I have never yet seen a good man who habitually shot with any semblance of haste.

I know several rabbit hunters who can connect quite consistently with their favorite quarry in places where I could not get in a shot, yet they all believe the reason why they cannot hit grouse is because they are not fast enough. "They're fifty yards away before I can get the gun to my shoulder," they will say; but let us see how that works out in figures. When a grouse gets up from underfoot and flashes off through the trees, one might think a conservative estimate of its speed would be at least a hundred miles per hour, but is actually less than half that. It varies with wind conditions and the extent of the bird's fright, but the average speed of a ruffed grouse is only forty miles per hour. That is fifty-eight and two-thirds yards each three seconds, and although you may swear to the contrary, it does not start out at full speed. The thunder of its wings lends that impression, but it is physically impossible for any bird to attain instantly its maximum velocity.

If your ruffed grouse appears to be in an unwarranted hurry to depart, you may be sure it is well aware of all the unpleasant things that can happen to it in that first half-second of its flight. I have killed scores of grouse in alder country where they must bounce almost straight upward for ten feet in order to clear the tops of the alders, and I have taken them, without unseemly haste, before they made that short distance.

I was shooting one day with a companion possessed of a very nervous temperament and also a fixed determination to take his share of the birds, when out from a circular patch of junipers not more than fifteen feet across we kicked a grouse which the dogs had missed. Its flight was entirely unexpected; we were walking along, side by side, with our guns tucked beneath our arms.

The bird got up from the center of the cover, less than ten feet from either of us, but on the side next to my companion, who went into action at the first flutter. I solemnly swear the bird had not fully emerged from the two-foot-high bushes before he loosed the first charge at it. He missed it cleanly, worked the action on his pump gun, and shot again just as the bird reached the edge of the juniper patch. It had traveled not an inch more than ten feet before the second shot.

This latter was also a miss, as I had expected it would be because of his haste; but the fellow was a fair shot when he could control his impetuosity, and I had not the slightest doubt he would kill the bird with his third and last shell.

I had been standing there watching him and thinking

how foolish one was to let even a ruffed grouse fluster him like that, and had made no move to raise my own weapon; but, when his third shot failed to connect, I drew the gun from under my arm, killed the bird, took thirty-two steps over the rough and uneven ground, and picked it up.

I remember another instance when, hunting alone, I started another bird under similar conditions. This one got up so near me that I could feel the air disturbance which her wings created at my feet, and started for a dense clump of spruces some thirty feet away. As though it had happened within the hour, I recall leveling the gun at her and waiting for what seemed minutes for her to get to the very edge of the spruces before I touched the trigger. I realized when the bird came down that she was still very close, and as I frequently do, I paced the distance as I went in to pick her up. This time, I took eight long steps and one short one, and stood above her.

So much, then, for speed. It is plainly apparent that grouse have not enough of it, or they would get away more often than they do. It is equally evident that the average man has far too much, or he would score more frequently than he does. That was the lesson I learned from those un-identified birds on the marshes, and that, too, marked a new era in my shooting.

The fellow who proposes to kill grouse or any other

game consistently, has a bigger job on his hands than merely finding a gun that fits him. I am not implying he should not try to do that, for if he has a good fit in the gun he finally chooses, he will have less of them because of it; but the thing on which he should center his energy is the mastering of the weapon.

Get any carpenter to show you his favorite hammer, and then ask him what he will take for it. He will say, "Why, I wouldn't sell it for a hundred dollars. Now, this hammer—" and then he will rave about the fit of the handle, and the way it hangs in his hand, and will show you how he can drive nails with it, even with his eyes closed. He will pass it over for your approval, and you will say, "Yes, that's certainly a nice one," and all the while you will be thinking: "Huh! He calls this thing a hammer!"

The reason why the carpenter likes it should be obvious to anyone. He has used it regularly for ten years, and it has become as much a part of him as the fingers which grip the handle. It may be clumsy and poorly balanced, but when he is called upon to do a workmanlike job, it is the tool he uses.

From the little, custom-made gun I learned that extreme lightness in the length of the barrels was a mistake, as was also the concentration of weight in the center. A magnetic needle is similarly balanced, and every sportsman knows how little movement is necessary to start the point whirling; but balance is something the prospective gun buyer need not worry about if he buys a standard weapon made by any good American gun company. Its engineers have worked out the solution to that problem long ago, and any changes you wish to make had best be conservative ones in drop of stock, height and width of comb, and pitch of heel.

Pitch, by the way, is something which many shooters seldom consider, and it is surprising how many are completely ignorant of the meaning of the term; but no matter how closely the measurements may approach your idea of perfection, if the pitch is wrong you are beaten, at least where accurate snap shooting in the brush is concerned.

Deciding upon the correct degree for his individual requirements is something which each shooter must determine for himself by a careful analysis of the way the gun performs while he is shooting at game. If the buttplate catches or drags against his clothing while the weapon is being thrown into position, or the comb does not invariably come firmly and smoothly up against the cheek and stop in exactly the same position each time, he may be pretty sure the angle of pitch is not great enough. A black-and-blue spot on the cheek, or a bloody nose, is indicative of the same fault.

If, on the other hand, after releasing the first shot, he finds that his face no longer cuddles firmly against the comb, and that the butt has slipped down on the shoulder, with a corresponding elevation of the muzzle, it is an assured fact that the pitch is too great; but if the recoil drives the weapon firmly but pleasantly straight back, and he finds on looking down the barrel that it still points where it did when he released the trigger, he can safely concentrate on making the second shot necessary less often.

Much has been said and written concerning swing and lead, and all manner of diagrams have been drawn depicting the manner in which one should elevate his gun to the line of flight and then swing ahead until he has caught and passed the bird; but if any brush shooters practice this method, I have never met them. The men of my acquaintance who consistently kill grouse and woodcock, do so with a minimum of effort, swinging the gun at an angle which will intercept the flight of the bird. To the last man they vehemently assert they never lead even a cross shot more than to be certain they are "up near the front end of her," which to my mind is pretty good evidence that one should learn to shoot by instinct rather than by mathematical calculations. In duck shooting, or other types of shooting of a similar nature, where game is killed at distances well up to the utmost possible range, I believe the reverse to be

LYNN
BOGUE
HUNT

true, for I have seen wildfowlers who apparently had the thing worked out to an exact science. In the brush, however, where one's best chances for the entire day are often no more than a momentary flash of brown against a background of green, one must hit by instinct in the majority of cases, or not at all.

My oldtime friend, Bill, was at once my despair and delight in those days when I looked upon him as the pinnacle of perfection where grouse shooting was concerned, for almost daily he executed hits so difficult that I thought no other man in the world could begin to approach his flawless artistry with a scatter gun. In later years I came to know that he spoke the truth when he said, "There ain't nothin' to it, Bub. All you got to do is look at the bird and pull the trigger." So far at least as guns are concerned, I think he spoke the truth, for it would be hard to find one that did not throw an effective pattern at the distance within which most grouse are killed, or one so poorly designed that a good wing shot could not master it with a few days' practice. I recall one fall when the mechanism of my brush gun went wrong in the midst of the shooting season, and I was obliged to fall back on my auto-loading trap gun which I had never previously used in the woods. The stock dimensions were one-and-a-half inches at both comb and heel, as compared to one-and-five-eighths and two-and-seven-eighths on the brush gun, yet I never shot more accurately than after the first half-day, although I did so with a conscious effort. Quite naturally, with so straight a stock, my tendency was to place the charge of shot too high, but as soon as I had taught myself to will it to go lower, it did so at once.

In the old days of night hunting for ducks on the marshes, the method of instinctive shooting also worked out to my advantage; and after I had become reasonably proficient in the art I could never detect any appreciable difference in my percentage of hits, whether the shooting was done in daylight, or on a night so dark that it was impossible to discern the targets unless they were very near, and well above the horizon line.

I have repeatedly killed ducks in baited pond-holes when the darkness was so intense that if I placed the gun to my shoulder I could not discern the slight disturbance in the water, which was my only clue to their whereabouts. On those occasions I held the gun at my side and pointed it entirely by instinct, and strange as it may sound, I do not recall a single occasion when I missed my mark. I also took one of my best bucks by that method. I had found a place where he came nightly in search of acorns, and arranged a little surprise party for him.

It had been dark for an hour when he came in, but I

had anticipated that, and had taken my stand in a narrow gully, in the fond hope that he might travel along the crest of the bank, where he would be outlined against the western sky.

I was a nervous wreck when he made his belated appearance, for I had heard him for a half hour, and my state of mind was not improved when I found, on raising the gun, that I could not discern him in the darkness. Dropping the gun to my side I leaned forward, and by straining my eyes to the utmost was just able to make out his silhouette against the sky, from which the last trace of light had departed. From where I sat, holding the gun in my hands and with my elbows resting on my knees, I gave him the right barrel, saw him leap forward, switched the gun ahead, pulled the other trigger—and got him with each charge, as was proven by the fact that I found ten buckshot in him although each shell contained but nine.

The game of skeet was originated to help prospective wing shooters, but I believe it has deteriorated to a certain extent since it has become such a highly competitive sport, in which the shooter takes every advantage the rules will allow; but one may learn much from it if he follows it for a single season.

To my mind, it does not even closely approximate any form of wing shooting, for the target loses speed rapidly rather than gaining or merely holding its own, but it is good practice nevertheless.

In the matter of skeet guns, however, science has taken a hand, and if one wishes to purchase the best thing obtainable, so far as ease of handling and effectiveness of pattern at short and medium ranges is concerned, he can do no better than go to some good gun store and make his selection from their stock of weapons designed especially for the shattering of targets on a skeet field.

Then, after he has shot a few thousand rounds through it, and has arrived at the conclusion his brush shooting is something to write home about, he will, if I may be permitted to judge from my own experience, run across a one-eyed octogenarian, armed with an antiquated gaspipe, who, with one hand tied behind his back, can shoot circles around him.

If it is possible to extract a single grain of consolation from the knowledge of the fact that the seasons are slipping past with ever-increasing rapidity, I think it will be found in the realization that if one has not gained wisdom, he has at least lost some of the fallacious reasoning of youth. The days I have spent afield are priceless, and I would not exchange the memory of them for all the lost wealth of the Incas, but I do wish my pockets contained some of the money I tossed away in those years while I was searching for a weapon which would overcome my faults. Not until later did I learn that not the least of my faults was my stubborn belief the gun was master, and man the servant; and I continued to pour such dollars as I could earn down the same well-worn hole. I was killing grouse then—an unusual number of them I now think, in view of the fact I was continually handicapping myself with every conceivable form of weapon—but I was far from satisfied with results. It was inevitable that such ponderous thinking as I did should eventually produce results, but I blush when I recall how many years were required for the truth to hammer its way into my sluggish brain. When that happy event took place I was twenty-eight years old.

# CHAPTER IV

BY this time, if any reader has followed me thus far, I suppose he will be looking up from his book and saying, "Humph! This fellow seems to be rather interested in ruffed grouse."

From those days when I sat at the edge of the big swamp and watched the birds come out on the oak ridges to feed, has been a far cry, but never for a single season since then have I been out of touch with them for many weeks at a time. It was my love for them which induced me quite early in life to respect the game laws concerning them, but nothing could keep me from continuing our intimate association. From the time of the first snows until the frosts of the next autumn, I haunted their retreats almost daily, spying upon them from secluded hide-outs, and prying into their private lives with all the lack of respect for privacy of a candid-camera enthusiast.

I am aware that some of my ornithological friends of feminine persuasion look upon me with disfavor, claiming among themselves that I am a ghoul and vampire, and that my interest in wildlife is based wholly upon my desire to destroy it; but no accusation was ever more false. I have a solicitous regard for all bird life. I recognize its value in our economic welfare, and I try so far as it lies in my power to protect it; but to the ruffed grouse I accord more humble homage than I can give to any other species, and with each passing year my respect and admiration for him grows greater.

Destined by nature forever to spend its days in a land of inclement weather, where winter temperatures often run far below zero, he has developed a physical stamina and a mental alertness far superior to that of any other bird I know.

To me, at least, it seems almost miraculous that any living creature can feed upon so diversified a diet for eight months of the year, and then immediately change to a single, restricted one, and thrive so well upon it as the grouse does when it starts budding. From the time it is hatched, in late April or early May, in my section of the country, it feeds voraciously upon a hundred different things of both the animal and vegetable kingdoms. Gradually, if the fall weather is normal, it necessarily changes more and more to a strictly vegetarian diet, but in the event of an unseasonal snowstorm it immediately begins budding, and continues to do so until spring is again well advanced.

In my early days I thought it not at all unusual to find half a dozen nests in that strip of woods which bordered the marshland, and once I had located them I watched over them with all the zeal of an Old World gamekeeper. My concern for them was of a more selfish nature then than now, for I looked upon them as creatures evolved for my especial benefit, and I came to have a violent antipathy toward anything which presumed to encroach upon my rights. Along the seacoast, crows had always been a problem to the farmer, but they soon learned they could not build with impunity in my vicinity. Much of the wooded area was swamp land, where, in some of the wettest portions, groups of tamaracks grew to a height and circumference I have never seen equaled elsewhere. In one of these groups, close down by the marsh, a band of blue herons nested each year, but in many of the others the black predators took up their arduous duties of housekeeping.

Cleverly constructed they were, in the very tops of those eighty-foot trees, and I suppose their builders thought them immune from molestation by anything without wings; but they little knew the mettle of the youngster whose prying eyes found them one by one. It was often a tussle to make the first ten or fifteen feet, but when I had won my way up into the lower branches I swarmed up as easily as a Norwegian sailor could have done. That I lived to tell about it can be attributed to good fortune rather than the exercising of any sort of judgment, for when I had once spotted a nest I went up to it there and then, irrespective of wind or weather.

The trees were as limber as willow wands, and with a good southeaster booming in from the ocean to add its power to my pendulum-like weight, they swayed in a fashion which, I fear, would have made my parents' hair stand on end had they known it; yet never but once did I suspect that my position might be a dangerous one.

It was late in the season when I discovered a nest which I had previously overlooked. I had heard the unmistakable calling of young crows, and after a stealthy approach I was rewarded at last by the sight of four black heads raised above the rim of a well-concealed nest.

They were, I found when I reached them, slightly more than half grown, and considerably more than half inclined to resent my intrusion, for they ruffled their immature feathers, and cawed hoarsely at me when I began pushing them from the nest to the ground below, where they could be more safely dispatched. I had dumped two of them unceremoniously over and was reaching for the third, when a black bombshell shot by my head so fast that I could feel the wind of its passing. With that, the fledglings in the nest set up a more raucous cawing, and suddenly the air around me was filled with crows, darting past me so close that the tips of their wings sometimes almost touched my clothing, and squalling in such a frenzy of anger and excitement as I had never heard.

[ 118 ]

To say that I was frightened is to put it mildly, for at best I could free only one hand, and I momentarily expected they would change their tactics and launch themselves at me *en masse*. Why they did not do so I have never been able to determine, for they were so carried away with the fierceness of their rage that I am sure they felt no fear, and they could easily have annihilated me without loss to themselves.

Hoping that it might distract their attention from me, I pushed the other two birds from the nest; but it was a mistake, for while many of them followed after the hapless victims, yet when I started precipitately down it seemed to rouse them to new heights of fury, and they flew back to harass me with redoubled vigor. Gaining the ground at last I fled ignominiously, leaving the young ones where they had fallen; but when I reached home I grabbed a gun and what shells I had, went back and had ten minutes of such crow shooting as I have never again been privileged to enjoy. Their excitement had partly abated, but when on my approach the youngsters again set up their clamor, they returned as fearlessly as before, and the echoing reports of the gun disconcerted them not at all.

It was barbarous, I suppose, but I have never regretted it, and it is the only type of shooting in which I still indulge for the mere sake of killing. It is my belief that the crow is

[ 119 ]

the greatest single enemy to bird life in New England, and I am more than half convinced that his depredations, during the nesting season, equal those of all others combined.

Unless one has seen them in their migrations he cannot imagine how staggering their totals must be. I have seen them flighting northward along the coast in late March, when there are hundreds of them in sight each minute of the day, from dawn to dusk, and oftentimes the flight lasts for a week. There are millions upon millions of them on that one route alone, with probably hundreds of other flights throughout the length and breadth of the land; and each one of the sly old renegades goes flitting silently about from tree to tree and bush to bush, seeking with those crafty eyes of his the nests of the lesser feathered folk who furnish him one of his staple articles of food.

That they have some means of communicating ideas I am quite firmly convinced, for it was not long before they shunned our strip of woods as though it were infested with a plague (as indeed it was), and the grouse were left to nest undisturbed. With the hatching of the flocks, my vigilance increased, and no poultry man ever felt his loss more keenly than I did when I found that fate had taken its toll among some of the vigorous little fellows.

Occasionally there was a year when the young birds seemed to possess unusual stamina, and the mortality among them was negligible. I remember finding one nest of twelve eggs in a secluded corner, and they not only all hatched, but the entire flock reached maturity, for I saw them several times each week from the day they emerged from their shells until early in the shooting season, and counted them frequently after they were large enough to make counting less difficult.

I used to wonder why their death rate varied so much from year to year, and attributed it principally to unseasonably cold weather and heavy rains, but I believe now that I was only partly right. Young grouse are active from the day they hatch, and are compelled to forage for their food, but in incredibly short time they grow feathers which will shed an ordinary rain and retain their bodily heat while doing so. Until this has been accomplished their mother's body affords ample protection against cold or any sudden shower; but a rain of several days' duration is bad medicine, even for young ducklings, unless an adequate amount of food is readily accessible. More than half the things on the menu of a young grouse are some forms of insect life, and the production of the latter is considerably upset by a prolonged rain. Twice in my life I have seen a large colony of full-grown purple martins all but wiped out by rains that lasted a week, and it is not hard to imagine what similar conditions can do to a flock of tiny grouse chicks.

On the other hand, I believe an excessive drought to be equally disastrous, for I have seen birds disappear in midsummer, after unusually good hatching seasons, and I have never been able to attribute the cause to anything but the unseasonable weather. It is quite generally known that many species of wildlife suffer a periodic decline, but I doubt if the cause has ever been rightly determined. To say they are wiped out by some dread disease, and to imply that it is Nature's method of preserving the stamina of the species through breeding only from the survivors does not appear to me to be sound logic, for I believe the tendency would be to produce offspring immune to the ill effects of the malady.

Also, I suppose, there is a readily discernible flaw in my theory that weather conditions are largely responsible, for they might be ideal in one section of the country, and bad beyond comparison in another, yet the same scarcity of birds would exist in each.

Invariably when legislation seems advisable to protect some species of wildlife, a fanatic will arise and plead tearfully that shooting be restricted. "Stop the shooting and the game will come back of its own accord," he will say; but it has never been so simple as that in my experience. Thousands upon thousands of shore birds lined our beaches in the old days, but although they have been on the protected list for a number of years, and although the open nature of the environment in which they are found is an effective check on poaching, their numbers have become less with each passing year.

Several years ago, the authorities in the state of Maine became alarmed at the scarcity of grouse, and made a drastic reduction in the length of the open season. Situated as I was, so near the border, it made little difference to me. I was sorry for the poor chaps who would be deprived of their favorite sport, but, I must admit, was just the least bit self-ishly pleased with my own good fortune. I could continue to shoot in New Hampshire, and when the increase in Maine again warranted it, I could once more enjoy something like the oldtime shooting.

If I remember correctly, the season was lengthened after three years and has not again been restricted; but while my regular hunting area extends nearly fifty miles from the border, and is fine grouse country, too, the shooting there was not so good as that which I had been finding in New Hampshire, or that which I could still find there. Curiously enough, it has never been as good since. I am not so foolish as to think the shortage was caused by restricting the shooting, but the thing didn't work out according to specifications.

In 1936 a closed season on grouse in New Hampshire

was seriously discussed, and I was approached by several persons who wished me to support the move. Once again I was in the same position as before. I could hunt in Maine without any inconvenience, and could probably find birds enough to satisfy my meager requirements, but I opposed the move, and I am entirely honest when I say I did so without any selfish motives. If by so doing I could bring grouse back in the oldtime numbers, I would hang my old gun in a place of honor above the mantel, and never kill another bird so long as I lived, but it is my opinion that if every hunter in the country did the same thing it would make very little difference. Whenever a periodic decline occurs it is quite uniform over large areas, and it is just as apparent in sanctuaries where food and water is abundant, and incessant warfare is waged on all predators, as it is in sections which are hunted the hardest.

One of the arguments used by the agitators for a closed season, was that 28,000 grouse had been bagged in the State the previous fall. With ready pad and pencil, they proceeded to prove for my enlightenment just what would have been the result had those unfortunate birds been spared. I must admit it worked out beautifully. Twenty-eight thousand birds were 14,000 pairs. Had they bred, each pair would have hatched ten chicks, of which five would have reached maturity, an increase of 250 per cent.

Of the old birds, half would have survived and bred the next year, which coupled with the product of the younger generation would have swelled the total to 175,000. "That's just two hatching seasons," they told me. "Those are the birds you could have hunted next fall if we hadn't killed off our breeding stock." I agreed, but told them they hadn't carried it far enough. I quoted Russia, and advocated a five-year plan. Then I got out my own pencil and paper and proved to them, by their own figures, that after the fifth hatching season the number of young birds to reach maturity would have been 1,640,625, with something like a half million old birds to sit around and give them friendly counsel. The sixth year we could market a million birds and still have more than four and a half million left for breeding stock. They went away in high dudgeon, vowing I had no common sense.

It reminds me of my neighbor who came down from the city armed with an array of figures and boundless enthusiasm, and entered into the poultry business. The sheriff sold him out at the end of four years, and just before he left to go back to the city, he came over to say good-bye.

"Son," he said to me, by way of parting advice, "if ever you get up against it and don't know which way to turn, remember there is money in the poultry business. I know. There's ten thousand of mine in it."

Propagating game, and particularly ruffed grouse, has not yet reached the stage where the increase can be successfully determined by a professor of mathematics. Some day the reason for the periodic decline will be found and grouse will be raised as easily as pheasants; and I believe it is in experimental work of this nature that a portion of the sportsman's money should be spent. The factors which seem to determine an assured increase of quail and pheasants are adequate food supplies and covers, especially in winter. Ducks need bigger and better breeding grounds, food, and common-sense restrictions in the concentration areas, but I fail to see how any of these things enter into our grouse problem. It is true that all of our old-growth timber is gone, and there was a time when I considered that largely responsible for the shortage, but I no longer believe it. It is quite true that heavy evergreen cover is an imperative necessity in the winter, but there is still enough of it to shelter ten times the present number of birds. The question of food or lack of it can hardly be considered seriously, for I have never known a season, even when the grouse population was at its highest peak, that there was not an abundance of readily available food.

One has but to consider the days when the passenger pigeon was in the height of its glory, to realize that an incredible amount of food exists. Audubon describes one flock of these birds that was more than a mile in width and that continued to fly in undiminished numbers for three days. He estimated the number of birds that passed him each three hours to be 1,115,136,000, and arrived at the conclusion they would consume the staggering total of 8,712,000 bushels of food each day. They ate some grain, to be sure, and paid for it dearly, but the greater part of all their food was found in the wild state, and it was essentially the same as that on which ruffed grouse feed for eight months of the year.

Since it is quite evident that lack of neither food nor adequate winter cover is responsible, I suppose the man who advocates abolishing the gun will chuckle with glee at the trap I have set for myself and into which I have blundered; but he has yet to convince me that he is right.

Within five miles of the small city in which I live, are two fine grouse covers. They are so good and so readily accessible that they are hunted daily throughout the season. On Saturdays, Sundays and holidays, a small army of gunners comb them from end to end, and boys armed with .22's prowl about them all summer, yet I have never known a year when those places did not contain as many grouse as any others of a comparable size in the State. It doesn't sound reasonable, but it is nevertheless true. The only explanation I can give is that predators are kept down to a minimum, and the grouse have all matriculated in the school of experience.

After forty years of intimate association with them, I am convinced that I know little about grouse, and my conviction is strengthened by an experience I had last summer.

Late one evening I had a long-distance call from a stranger in another part of the State. He asked if he were talking with Mr. Spiller, and if I were the author of *Grouse Feathers*. I admitted the former, but hedged cautiously on the latter, inquiring, instead, if he had read it. Upon receiving an affirmative reply and his hearty assurance that he was still all right, I accepted the responsibility, and asked in what way I could be of assistance to him.

He told me a rather pretty fairy tale of a ruffed grouse that came out of the woods to hobnob with the hired men as they worked in the field, causing them no end of bother. The bird, he claimed, would come to his whistle in the woods and eat from his hand. He wished to know if I cared to come and see it.

I was not very keen about it, for I seriously doubted its being a ruffed grouse. A spruce partridge, perhaps, or someone's tame hen-pheasant, but a grouse—no! The thing was contrary to their every instinct. It just couldn't happen. Still, the fellow had a pleasant voice, and seemed to know what he was talking about, and before I hung up

I had made arrangements to visit him the next afternoon.

My wife's chief hobby, I sometimes think, is that of announcing the time at regular ten-minute intervals each morning, a procedure which, I believe, is intended to imply that my duty is to arise and provide a dab of butter for our daily bread; but her next great ruling passion is the study of birds. She was overjoyed when I broke the news to her, but I explained that seeing grouse was a man's job, requiring both caution and infinite patience, and if there did chance to be anything in the story it would be necessary for me to hide in some secluded place and view the enlightening spectacle from a distance. I did relent, however, to the extent of promising that she might accompany me, provided she would agree to stay in the car and keep as quiet as it is possible for a woman to do.

She readily agreed, but when we reached our destination she took matters in her own hands, firing questions at our host with the rapidity of a machine gun, and concluding the barrage by asking if she might accompany us.

"Why, certainly!" he said. "It won't make a bit of difference. Come right along."

He led us down through a field and into the woods for fifty yards, where he halted and began whistling softly, interspersing the liquid notes at intervals with stentorian calls of "He-re Susie! Co-me Susie!"

I had never heard such an unorthodox way of calling any creature of the wild, and was smiling skeptically to myself, when I heard a distant patter of feet upon the leaves, and, looking in its direction, saw a full-grown female grouse, with neck outstretched in token of her haste, running toward us as only a grouse can run.

At a distance of ten feet she halted and surveyed us shrewdly, her eyes, I thought, being particularly centered upon the dress the for-once speechless lady wore; but when our host moved slightly to one side and knelt among the leaves and pine needles, the bird came up to him unhesitatingly and pecked at the bit of apple he held toward her.

Quite overwhelmed for a minute or two, I at last recovered sufficiently to unsling my camera and get into action. The light beneath the trees was poor, and I was looking speculatively up at the sky when my newly found friend asked if I would prefer to have the bird out in the field. This was heaping miracle upon miracle, but I had sufficient breath left with which to say yes.

"All right," he said. "Go out and wait by that pile of cold-frames, and I will call her out."

We had scarcely reached them when, choosing a more direct route, he came into view with the bird trotting at his heels like a well-trained dog.

Then ensued such an hour as I had never expected to see, for the bird had no more fear of us than if we had been members of her kind. Within five minutes from the time she entered the field she was pecking at a piece of apple held between my fingers. I went to the edge of the woods and gathered several ripe blackberries and raspberries which she also took from between my thumb and forefinger. Spying a laden raspberry bush some fifty feet away, I hurried to it, bent it over in order to break it off, and as I did so the bird stepped up on my shoes and began plucking the ripe fruit.

The most peculiar phase of the whole thing, to my mind, was the fact that the bird was not forced by hunger to approach us. The strip of woods in which she had made her home for the summer comprised about twelve acres, and there were no other grouse in it. Food was everywhere, in quantities sufficient to feed a score of her kind, and she was as plump and sleek as any grouse I have ever seen.

She was boisterously playful, brushing about my feet, jumping up to peck at my wife's dress, and pouncing upon my hands exactly as a playful kitten would do when I ran them through the grass before her.

All wild creatures have a look in their eyes which those who have accepted man as master do not have; but there was no trace of it in hers after those first moments in which she paused to look us over. Yet after an hour of riotous fun,

[ 131 ]

and just as she was again getting set to launch herself forward at my hands, I saw her stop suddenly and stretch her neck as stiffly as though it were made of steel, while the tiny topknot on her head snapped erect, and the bright, hard look came into her eyes. I have never seen another transformation so swift or so utterly complete. In the briefest of seconds she had become a creature of the wild once more, and emitting a characteristic *Cur-rew* of alarm, she turned and stole softly off toward the wood, setting her feet down cautiously, and peering back toward us with one bright and beady eye.

Watching her closely, I decided after a moment that her gaze was not centered upon us. I turned and looked behind me, and there on a hilltop, two hundred yards away and sharply outlined against the flawless sky, I beheld that combination which used to strike terror to the hearts of those other grouse of the long ago: the age-old, happy combination of a small boy and his dog.

I came home, fired with enthusiasm, and quite convinced I had just seen the eighth wonder of the world, but when I took the matter up with my good friend Ray Holland, I was crestfallen to learn that it was something which was reported almost annually.

I again displayed my ignorance about grouse the last time I was in Quebec. We arrived at our outfitters late in the day and decided to postpone our departure for the interior until early morning. At dinner that evening we were served canned partridge breasts which were as delicious as anything I had ever tasted. Although I was an alien in a strange land, and was obliged to converse chiefly by gestures, I at once began to feel at home, for here was something with which I was entirely familiar. Later, I hunted up our head guide and gesticulated wildly at him in an attempt to learn if I had been eating "spruce" partridge. I got the question home to him at last but failed miserably in understanding his answer. He repeated it, then when I still failed to comprehend, retreated into another part of the house, from which he presently emerged, bearing a large and excellently mounted specimen of a male ruffed grouse.

"Birch," he said, and I agreed.

"You shoot him?" I asked then, trying to lead the conversation around so that I would have an opportunity to air my knowledge.

"No shoot," he replied. "Take with snare."

"I know how that is done," I said, and proceeded to impart to him all the information I had gathered concerning snares, setting an imaginary row of stakes across the floor, and arranging a noose cunningly in the opening. He shook his head in disapproval, when I had finished.

"No do that way," he denied, and explained how they

rigged up long spruce poles, with screw eyes for guides and a piece of stiff wire for a line, and snared the unsuspecting birds by dropping the noose over their heads and pulling it tight, much as the irresponsible Kiko used to snare pickerel in the river down home.

Poor Joe! He had never seen a bird dog, and knew absolutely nothing about our method of hunting grouse. I explained the system to him as best I could, and tried to fire the telling with some of my own enthusiasm, but he only shook his head sadly when I had finished.

"Too bad!" he said, thinking, I suppose, of the tremendous amount of effort involved, and pitying me because I had never known the thrill of creeping up behind an unsophisticated bird and garroting it with a bit of wire.

Our systems were different, but I could not say that his was unsportsmanlike. Similarly, I no longer condemn the man whose favorite sport is hunting grouse in trees. Although I have never had the pleasure of participating in it I can readily understand how hunting with a good "tree" dog could be fine sport. Certainly, in most parts of New England, one's bag would be considerably less than that of an experienced wing shot, and it is not for me to say it is taking an unfair advantage of the bird. I am convinced, too, that the fellow who depends upon "still hunting" is entitled to all the grouse he may take. If he is woodsman enough to steal up and get a shot at a feeding bird, or so observant that he can accurately mark its flight and then locate it in the profusion of branches where it has taken refuge, he has done something of which any man might well be proud. I am not overly enthusiastic, though, about the fellow who believes every method to be fair so long as it meets with success. I speak with authority when I say there is little of sportsmanship, and far less of satisfaction, in the killing of sitting birds after one has achieved even a minimum of success in wing shooting. It took some time for me to come to that conclusion—and yet more time to break the habit I had formed in my youth—but I am master of it at last. If a grouse hops up into a tree when I step in front of my dog, I'll toss my hat at her to drive her out, and then bag her if I can, but those who sit on stone walls, or dust themselves fearlessly in the road before my car, can continue to do so without interference from me.

Bit by bit, too, I am trying to school myself to shoot only at those birds which my dog has pointed. It is a far harder task than the other, for in order to accomplish it I find it necessary to forget all those things I struggled so long to learn, and which at last have become purely instinctive with me. If any man smiles tolerantly and thinks I am a weak-minded simpleton, he does not know much concerning anatomy and nerve reflexes. It requires long training for a boxer to learn to keep his eyes open when he sees a whistling left jab traveling toward them, and it also requires a rather complete mastery of oneself to refrain from swinging the gun on a grouse that hammers out unexpectedly from underfoot, especially if one has devoted more years than he likes to count to the task of making that action as instinctive as the drawing of one's breath.

If the only satisfaction to be derived from the sport lay in killing birds, I would have quit the game long since. I do not deny it is a stirring and logical climax to that which preceded it, but the good shots I have made and the worthwhile bags I have brought home, are the things which are the dimmest in my memory. I recall the story of an old fisherman who, years before, had taken a record catch of trout from a stream. Asked to recount it for the benefit of some of the younger generation, he pondered long before he replied:

"I can't remember much about it, excepting that I took some nice trout. Some of the biggest ones ever caught around here, I guess. But I do recall after I'd fished through the meadows I lay down to rest under a big pine on the bank. There was a smell of arbutus in the air, and while I lay there, kind of dreamin', a little brown bird came and lit on my hat."

Queer, is it not? Out of infinite nothingness those trout

had taken shape. They had lived for a time, and served their purpose gloriously for a few brief moments, but they were long since gone and forgotten. Only the wild, sweet scent of arbutus remained—and the memory of a companionable and fearless little wood warbler.

It is on pages such as these that my past is spread before me. I killed hundreds of ducks in my boyhood, yet as I strive to recall the circumstances it is not the plummet-like descent of their stricken bodies I see, nor do I hear in fancy the soul-stirring thud as they crash down upon the water. Memory paints, rather, a picture of the frost-browned grasses, with the sea wind stirring them into undulating motion, and the cloud shadows chasing one another interminably across them. I smell their salty sweet tang once more, and hear again the murmur of the distant ocean and the gentle lapping of the tide waters among the tules along the river bank.

In like manner do I remember my grouse-hunting days. Quite frequently my shooting companion will say, as we are driving along:

"Remember the time we took our limit in here at our right?" Sometimes I am able to recall the incident readily, but more frequently I am obliged to confess I have forgotten.

"Sure, you can remember it," he will say then. "That

was the day when Duke was gone so long, and we found him lying down, in there by the old hemlock."

I recall it then, vividly. The sudden realization that the tinkle of old Duke's bell had ceased, and the guilty knowledge that I had not been paying sufficient attention to remember where I had last heard the sound. The fact that we bagged ten grouse that day was buried in the limbo of forgotten things, but still fresh in my mind was the poignant recollection that Duke was getting to be an old dog, and a sudden fear that his champion's heart would never again force his weary legs through another cover. We hunted half an hour before we found him, and through every cursed minute of it the dread of what we might find was stabbing at my soul. Can I ever forget the moment when my eye detected that white spot under the hemlock, or the queer feeling of angry relief I felt as I hurried over? The old rascal was neither dead nor ill, but when his legs had tired from the strain of pointing the grouse which still crouched closely in the shadows, he shrewdly let them fold up beneath him, and with head outstretched across a fallen limb, still calmly pointed his bird, and as calmly waited for us to find him.

"Yes," I say, as it all comes back to me. "I remember it now. That was the last fall we hunted Duke. The next season we started your Bob."

"Not Bob," he contradicts, "but Dime. That little white setter that I bought down in Alabama. Queer, about that dog. I don't know whether it was her nose or what. Remember the time we were up in the Allen cover with her, and she—"

He pauses to chuckle softly, and I laugh with him, then listen with only half my mind as he recounts the incident, for I am trying to recall an unimportant thing which I had forgotten.

"That grouse that old Duke was pointing?" I ask. "Did I kill her or did you?"

"I killed her," he replies. "She broke behind the hemlock. Don't you remember? You were stooping over the dog, and she came out from behind that bunch of laurel?"

"I recall that part of it," I answer, "but I had forgotten about the bird."

I presume the state of its executioner's mind as he went about his task would make little difference to a stricken grouse, even if it were aware of it, and I am glad the present day sportsman's attitude has changed from that of the old-time Englishman's who was reputed to have said, as he looked out upon a sun-bathed and newly washed world: "By Jove! What a ripping morning! Let's go out and kill something." That our point of view has changed, I firmly believe. There are, and always will be, I suppose, a certain number of people in whom a sense of fair play has never developed, and youth is always impetuous and prone to chafe at every restraint, but the majority of sportsmen realize that the day of big bags and unrestricted limits is irrevocably gone, and that only by the practice of wise conservation can future sport be assured.

Personally, I am glad because of the reduction in daily limits on most species of game, and as far as grouse are concerned I would not ask to see it changed, in my State at least, from the present maximum of four. In the old days when the blue sky and the capacity of one's shooting coat were the only limits, there was no gauge or standard by which to measure success. Bill Brown might come in some night with ten birds, and yet the day had been spoiled for him because he had not tied Joe Doakes' record of fourteen. And I fumed and fretted all the season because my high score of five proved that I was only half as good as Bill. But with an arbitrary limit of four, I can say—and make myself believe it, too—"Hm-mph! I could take that number any day if I cared to get out and hustle for them the way I used to."

Then, too, four grouse are enough for any average family. Often, in years gone by, more than the present season-limit of birds hung in my cellar at one time. Frequently it was a problem to dispose of them, for as delicious as they are when properly cooked, relatively few non-sporting families appreciate their delicate flavor, and I had the uncomfortable feeling at times that my gifts were not accepted with any too much enthusiasm. But if I give away a brace of birds now, I do so because I like the person and wish him to share my good fortune.

If anyone had told me when I was twenty-one that the time would ever come when I would voluntarily leave my gun in the car, and hunt all day with a camera, I would have called him something far less complimentary than "prophet," yet I have done it frequently each season for a number of years. That type of hunting does something to a fellow which is good for his soul. No matter how thick the cover, or how brief a glance I get at the bird, if it is within reasonable range it would be a dead one had I brought the gun along. There is no evidence of fevered haste, no snapping the gun halfway up and loosing a charge haphazardly into the surrounding atmosphere. No, a fellow takes his time, picks the spot where the bird will break into clear view, levels his forefinger at it, crooks it at the psychological moment, says "Bang!" and scores an unfailing, mental bull's-eye.

There's something about the feel of a gun in one's hands that has a tendency to rob him of his power of reason, and I'll venture to say there are but few of us who could not

learn more about our favorite quarry if we would only forget the gun for a time and devote our attentions to the
things which are of as much importance as the actual
shooting.

After all, the ability to hit any target is only half the
game. The essential difference between the fellow who sits
at the top of the ladder and the one who clings precariously
to a rung halfway up, is not in the percentage of hits each
makes, but in his ability to change an almost impossible
chance into one quite easily possible. After killing grouse
for twenty-five years, my old friend Bill arrived at the following conclusion: "If you can conniver around so as to
get a shot at half the birds you start, you're doin' as well as
any man can expect. Then if you kill half of them you
shoot at, you're doin' a darn sight better'n most of the folks
you run across."

I am thoroughly convinced that Bill was not far wrong
in his estimate, for while I am acquainted with hunters who
claim greater efficiency than that, I shall require something
more definite in the way of proof than their sworn affidavit
before I swallow the statement. No one day's score, nor
yet that of a single week can determine it, but if a truthful
tally of the empty cases is checked against the season's bag
it will pretty accurately determine the percentage of hits.

It is a natural tendency for one to look for a bird immediately in front of his pointing dog, and from what I have observed, it is equally natural for one to go blindly in and kick the bird out, trusting to the fickle goddess of luck to influence it to fly in the open. Such a course may serve to prove whether one shoots indifferently or well, but it never even half approximated all the possibilities of bird hunting. There is a satisfaction about being right that far exceeds any elation one may feel because he was merely fortunate, and for me at least, the greater part of the fun lies in trying to determine the location of the bird, picking out its probable line of flight, and getting into a position where I will have a reasonable chance of intercepting it.

My schooldays were spent principally either in idle dreaming or in endless waiting for the sound of the closing bell, but I do recall that more than one teacher reiterated fretfully, for my benefit alone, the truism that "Whatever is worth doing at all is worth doing well." I concurred heartily with their point of view, but it was the only common ground on which we could meet, for they invariably cherished the idea that several things were worthy of accomplishment, while I had narrowed the field down to only one. The saying, though, is worthy of a place in any sportsman's text book, and to none of them is it more directly applicable than to a grouse hunter.

That hunting a new cover is largely a matter of guesswork, I will freely admit, but the fellow who goes through it even once without learning many things which should work out for his benefit, is a mighty dull scholar. My observance of the feeding grouse at the edge of the old swamp led me, even in my early days, to believe that mature birds customarily follow a definite routine. If the feed is adequate they remain in a single restricted area often for a month at a time, feeding over the same range each day, and roosting in the same spot—and quite frequently on the same limb—each night. When danger threatens, their natural instinct is to seek refuge in heavy cover, a heritage from those ancestors who played the game of life or death long before shotguns constituted one of their problems. If there is a patch of dense evergreens in the immediate vicinity you may be assured your grouse knows its exact location, and you may be equally sure it will start directly for it if no hindering factors prevent its doing so.

Once in a blue moon, a fellow will stumble upon a bird that is quite unaware of his proximity, and in that event it gets up without the slightest idea where it is going, but at all other times it knows exactly what it intends to do. Because you cannot see the bird, is no evidence at all that it cannot see you. You are a hundred times larger, and it is at least an even chance that it is watching your every movement.

Let us assume from the fact that the dog is still staunchly holding his point, that the bird is either a young or an unsophisticated one; and let us try to figure out what prompts it to do whatever it does. It knows its own location exactly, and where the heavy cover is, too. Standing as rigidly as your statuesque dog, it watches him with one eye and you with the other, or if you are hidden from its view, listens keenly to the sound of your footsteps. So far the grouse is the master of the situation, for spread before its mind's eye is a clearly defined map, with accurately traced routes, and all danger points marked in red.

Until you came crashing into the scene, the game had been between the dog and the bird, but now the dog passes out of the picture and you take up where he has left off. So long as he remains motionless the grouse pays him no further attention. It may, perhaps, have even forgotten his existence, for fertile though it unquestionably is, the mind of a ruffed grouse persists in running on a one-way track. It knows quite definitely where you are, even though you may be hidden from view for the moment, but the one thing it does not know about you is that you suspect its presence, for this, remember, is the credulous type of bird that lies closely to a dog. If you start directly toward it, not much imagination on its part is required to know that the time for departure is at hand. Your dog, if he be good, has established a deadline across which you can seldom step without flushing your quarry if you are moving directly toward it, but if your direction is such that it appears you may pass it by on one side or the other, your chance of approaching yards nearer is considerably greater. To a certain extent ruffed grouse still rely upon their protective coloration, and they are reluctant to fly unless they deem it absolutely necessary.

The game then, as I like to play it, is to decide which way the fidgety young fellow prefers to take, and lay my plans accordingly. If I am familiar with the cover I have a fair idea of the location of the place it considers a safe haven, but my action is largely determined by the nature of the surroundings.

If we are near the edge of a large opening, I know the bird will go that way only as a last resort. Frequently under such conditions it will come straight for me if I approach from the side on which the heavy cover grows, but more often in that case it will start at a right angle from me, sometimes directly back over the dog, but more frequently straightway from him for a short distance, and then in a curving flight that will bring it back to the thick growth it has had in mind for minutes.

Should I chance to be hunting with a companion the problem is simplified considerably, for the fellow whose turn it is to shoot can circle around to the side on which the thicket grows, take his stand where he can get a fairly open shot in either direction, face the bird and wait while the other drives it out to him; but when one is alone the game is more complicated.

In that event, I know three things which should work in my favor. I have a more or less accurate knowledge of the bird's location, I know it will not fly by preference toward the open country, and I know, from the memory of a thousand other such experiences, that it will try immediately to place some obstruction between us as soon as possible after it takes to the air. So much is common knowledge which practically every bird shooter shares, but the use I make of it is, I believe, the yardstick by which to measure my ability, for there are no hard and fast rules to help me. No previous experience can help with this problem, for, like all those in the past and all the others to come, it is an individual one that must be solved then or never, and the oftener I can answer it correctly the greater is my chance of success, whether I be a good marksman or a poor one.

Each man has his own opinion and is entitled to it, but I could never convince myself that noise had much to do with speeding a bird's departure. Certainly, except on rare occasions, no hunter can move so silently that his presence is unsuspected, and I have no reason to believe a noisy approach is more alarming than a cautious one, especially if the latter is accompanied by the occasional crash of a bit of breaking wood underfoot, that echoes through the surrounding stillness as startlingly as the noise of a midnight prowler tripping over the perambulator downstairs.

If the hunter is far enough away, or if the nature of the surroundings hides him from the eyes of the grouse, the sound of his movements is the only clue of his whereabouts, and no one can blame a bird for becoming panicky when it imagines an enemy is creeping stealthily toward it. After I have made my decision concerning the location of the bird and the line of flight I hope to influence it to take, I'll rely on a steady approach to win over a hesitating one. I know I cannot approach noiselessly, so my only caution in that respect will be to avoid any startlingly sudden crash of breaking branches. I will try to make the bird think there is a strong possibility that I will pass by at a distance of twenty feet, but if I am so fortunate as to reach the spot I have in mind it will learn in short order that it was mistaken.

If the cover is thick enough before it, the chances are about ten to seven that its flight will be over the obstruction, but if it is of a more open nature it will almost certainly make for the nearest protecting screen and try to put it between us. The true test of my ability as a grouse hunter is answered by whether or not I have judged all the factors correctly. If the bird breaks into the opening I have picked, and if half its companions do the same throughout the season, I am a successful grouse hunter. The fact that I may kill them all, or miss them all, affects my status in that respect not at all. It merely proves my ability as a marksman.

Some years ago, when the season limit was fifty birds, circumstances arose which prevented me from entering the woods until twenty shooting days had passed. My hunting companion that year was a fine marksman, my equal in upland shooting, and my superior at many other kinds; but he had not had so much experience as I on grouse. Shooting alone for the first twenty days he had bagged thirty-five birds, but at the close of our sixth day together my score exceeded that of his for the entire season. It was not the fault of his shooting but merely that, although we were hunting side by side, I could outguess him at the ratio of five to one. Shortly afterwards, he made a public statement that no grouse in the county would even consider alighting until it had hunted me up and tried, at least once, to fly before me, but he retracted it a few years later. His shooting had not improved appreciably in the interim, but he had learned how to shoot grouse, and thereafter was perfectly capable of holding his own in almost any company.

To me, grouse shooting will always be a fascinating game because, as in chess, each move presents a new problem. I have long since passed the stage where my errors cause me the oldtime chagrin, but I wish I were able to solve some of the riddles which still baffle me.

I have never been able to determine why grouse will be so wild in one cover for weeks, and then, when one has gone half-heartedly back there some day, will lie as closely as woodcock. All manner of theories have been advanced as the reason, but I have not yet heard one that sounded logical to me, or that I could not disprove a dozen times each season.

It is commonly believed that grouse are unusually nervous on a windy day, the supposition being that the accompanying noise makes them over-fearful that an enemy is stealing upon them; but the best season's shooting I have enjoyed in the past twenty years was one fall when a strong northwest wind roared down through our foothills for twenty-eight consecutive days. No other meteorological condition can put me so out of sorts. I can accept either excessive heat or cold with equanimity, and bear a three days' rain with commendable fortitude, but creaking branches and scudding leaves always arouse a feeling of resentment within me; yet try as I would on that occasion, I could not maintain even a fair semblance of ill humor, for the birds lay beautifully from the first day, and continued to do so as long as the wind persisted.

Probably every trout fisherman has read or heard something concerning the "Solunar Theory," but not every gunner is aware that it has also been applied to grouse hunting. How anyone can spend days on end fishing a trout stream without securing a single rise, and still believe that the fish feed each time the ocean tide changes, is more than I can comprehend, although I am sure he has my permission to do so if he chooses; but to tell me that the full of the moon can in any way affect my score on grouse, is nothing more or less than a waste of time.

During the winter months, when they are forced to subsist on buds, grouse feed quite regularly in the early morning, and again just before dusk; and if there is anywhere in the world a place where tides consistently conform to that schedule I have yet to learn of it. Throughout the remainder of the year, they begin feeding in the morning and continue to do so intermittently throughout the day, gorging most heavily in the late afternoon, until their crops are stuffed to capacity and swelled to a size approximately that of a baseball. That this procedure is as fixed and as easily determinable as the ebb and flow of the tides I will readily admit, but my imagination is not fertile enough to link the two together by even the finest of threads.

Granting for the sake of argument that it may be true, I still reserve the privilege of asking, "What of it?" Does its sponsor wish me to believe grouse have the power of becoming invisible the moment they cease feeding, or that they can so withhold their scent that a dog cannot discern it? Or is he trying to persuade me that only at ebb tide will a charge of shot penetrate their feathers? He may know the answers, but I don't. I only know that it doesn't make sense.

I have never been able to explain, even to my own satisfaction, the reason for the so-called "crazy period" among grouse, although most men who are familiar with them are aware that it does exist. Occurring as it does in the early fall when feed is abundant, it can hardly be attributed to that, nor can the question of mating be seriously considered, yet grouse do fly and wander into all sorts of strange places during a brief period, although for what purpose I doubt if even they know.

Similarly, I cannot fathom the reason for their gathering into large flocks late in the season. Certainly it is not a system devised for mutual protection, for the greatest guarantee against danger that any grouse can have is its ability to remain hidden from its enemies. Again, the question of food can hardly enter into the problem, for the concentration frequently occurs when feed is abundant and birds relatively scarce.

In *Grouse Feathers*, I suggested that it might possibly be the faint recurrence of a long-lost instinct to migrate, and although what I said was wrongly interpreted by a few, I still maintain it is as plausible a reason as any other I have heard. Nothing was farther from my thought than to imply I believed they did migrate, but I know that during certain seasons in the fall their movements are actuated by a different impulse than that which guides their wanderings through the rest of the year.

In the fall of 1936, which, by the way, was a season of extreme scarcity in eastern New Hampshire and southern Maine, I again stumbled on a flock of grouse so large that their numbers could not be accounted for by cold logic or any ordinary hunting experience. It happened in typical grouse country, in a big area of mixed growth, which three of us, accompanied by two dogs, had combed quite thoroughly for several hours without finding even a lone single.

Then, within a hundred yards of the car, on the way out, from a corner where two score stately old pines grew, there came the sudden thunder of many wings, and I looked up to see grouse going across the opening which bordered the road, in a fan formation that stretched from east to south, while from the high tree tops above us they pounded their separate ways well around into the west.

To say that it impressed me as being unusual is to put it mildly, yet it was far easier to understand than were several other things about the incident.

[ 153 ]

As I have said, we were hunting with two dogs. Neither of them was mine, but both of them had been shot over rather extensively, and one of them I rated as being somewhat better than the average. Either of them was capable of winding single birds under favorable conditions at a distance which would have caused a novitiate to gasp in unbelief; yet they roaded in there where one would imagine the scent to be so strong that we could detect it ourselves, and bumped the flock without indicating a foreknowledge of their presence by so much as even a momentary change of pace.

I do not know why, when they should have been scattered either singly or in groups of two or three over several hundred acres, that every last bird in that territory should have gathered under those few pine trees or among their branches. Surely no threatened danger could have caused it, for no human ingenuity could have devised a plan that would have successfully herded them into so small an area.

Neither do I know why they arose as a single unit, for such is not their ordinary custom, yet although we went hopefully and carefully into every nearby place of possible concealment, we found not one lone straggler. That fact alone may be explained by saying that this was just one of the times when they all happened to go at once, but it does not shed any light on what took place afterward, for although I pride myself on my ability to mark down several birds that have taken a simultaneous but different direction of flight, and though I would have sworn I could strike out from where we stood and start a dozen different ones in half an hour, without the help of anybody's dog, I state nothing but the wholly incredible truth when I say that although the five of us combed every logical hiding place for two solid hours thereafter, we found not one grouse, nor did the dogs once indicate there was one within a thousand miles of us. Undoubtedly there is an answer to this one, too, but it just happens that I don't know what it is.

There is another thing only faintly connected with it, and yet it but serves to add to my confusion. Several years before the incident I have related, my shooting companion and I were in the same territory. It is a fine cover, large enough for half a day's shooting, and we had gone over it a few days previously with fair success. On this morning, however, we had found no birds. Coming out into the road a half mile below where the later event occurred, we discussed the situation and decided to go elsewhere. We had covered about half the distance which separated us from the car when, without any telltale thunder to apprise us of its coming, a grouse scaled across the road before us, on set wings, and planed down to a landing in a bit of thick growth some two hundred yards away.

"I wonder what started her out," my companion said. "Must be somebody else in there."

My interest in the closeness of another hunter did not begin to match that which I felt concerning the proximity of even one grouse, therefore I suggested that we go over and gather her in. He agreed half-heartedly, and we went after her. Now here is the curious thing about it. Without any cause which we have ever been able to determine, that bird had come in from some outlying point and flown directly to the patch of woods before us. We entered it, and for about ten minutes enjoyed such fast and furious shooting as I have seen neither before nor since. When the smoke had cleared away and the last bird had departed, we counted up and found that eight of their number reposed in our shooting jackets. I wish someone would explain what induced them to bunch up in that half-acre of ground—and then I would like to have him tell me how that one lone grouse knew they were there.

Many, many times I have seen grouse rocket up through the trees, far ahead of the dog, yet when we have marked their course and followed them up, I have known them to lie so closely before the dog that I have had no trouble at all in seeing them, and oftentimes found it necessary to go in and almost literally kick them out. I wonder whether it is reason or the lack of it that impels them to do so. It is not at all unusual to see a grouse make a short flight and alight in a neighboring tree, but when the same bird does no more than to stand there and bob its head inquisitively as it peers down upon your efforts to dislodge it with convenient sticks or stones, I admit that such mental processes as it may have are beyond my understanding. In direct contrast, though, to that foolhardy and witless procedure, I think its well known trick of flying directly toward the late afternoon sun is a mark of intelligence of the highest order, for a man must indeed have an eagle eye if he can see to shoot accurately under such circumstances.

No other American game bird has such an assortment of tricks at its ready disposal, and no other is so versatile in its manner of flight. If it deems that method of departure essential to its welfare, a grouse can hop up on a stump or stone and take off from there with only the slightest of betraying sounds. It has the power, and quite frequently the inclination, to catapult itself almost straight upward with all the speed and disconcerting air disturbance of a two-dollar skyrocket; and then again, though its departure may be accompanied by the same thunder of wings, it will make haste so slowly that, if one were so inclined, he could lay down his gun, turn a cartwheel, pick the weapon up and still have ample time in which to get his bird.

A grouse can—and all too frequently does, in alder or

birch country where the cover is not dense enough to provide the screen it desires—zoom upward at a forty-five
degree angle in a course as straight as that of a tightly
stretched wire, and then as it reaches the point toward
which you have been leisurely swinging, veer so sharply a
few feet either to the right or left that the charge of shot
goes exactly where he hoped it would. In the same type of
country it will take off and fly at full speed not more than
three feet above the ground, dodging in and out among tree
trunks by alternately twisting its fan-like rudder from left
to right, and seldom indeed will it touch so much as a
branch with the tip of a wing, but if its course happens to
bring it to an open field which it decides to cross, it may
fly head-on into the side of a house or barn, or decapitate
itself neatly upon a strand of telephone wire.

One day it will either lie well for your dog or take to
the air immediately when it discovers it is being pursued,
but on the next it may run ahead, through one thicket after
another for minutes, and stop only when it has reached an
opening which it fears to cross, or a bit of thick cover that
it has had in mind from the first.

I believe there are two senses of equal importance without which no man can ever become a good grouse shot.
The first is an abnormally keen sight, and the second is an
equally keen hearing. The mere ability to see the bird is

not enough when one is learning the game, although if he has learned to shoot more or less instinctively the natural dimming of his sight by age will not make the difference it otherwise would. Nevertheless, as any workman knows, he loses some of his efficiency when he is no longer able to see his work clearly, and the killing of grouse most certainly ranks as skilled labor.

I have shot with several trapshooters who claimed that under favorable conditions they could see their charge of shot an instant before it either hit or missed the target. Trying to prove to my own satisfaction if they were right or wrong, I have caught a flash of a bunched, gray cloud that seemed to cover the disc as it started to disintegrate. Whether or not it was the shot pattern I have no way of proving, and if it were, I do not know whether they saw it more clearly than I; but I do know they were mighty good trapshooters, and I do know that the clearness with which a moving object may be discerned varies tremendously among different people.

Many and many a time while a grouse was in the act of falling before my gun, I have called to my companion, "Left wing broken!" or "Right wing broken!" or, occasionally, "She's hit in the head!" and I have been correct a far greater number of times than I have been wrong. On dozens of different occasions I have designated the sex of birds that got up before me, and if my method of determining it is correct, I do not recall a time when my vision has played me false.

My assumption has never been scientifically corroborated, but I have always been led to believe that the black band which encircles the outer portion of the tail is unbroken on the male grouse, while on the female the bar is either absent from or only faintly discernible on the two feathers in the center of the fan. Although some claim there is no method other than an autopsy by which to determine sex, I still think I can distinguish between a mature cock and hen by neck ruff and conformation alone; and I have never examined what my judgment told me was a female without finding those two neutral colored tail feathers, nor have I ever seen what I believed to be a male upon whom the band was not unbroken.

When, with the sun playing upon its back, a bird angles steeply up before one at a reasonably short distance, every shade of marking stands out distinctly. The rudder-like tail is fully extended, and if two of the black bars are missing, their absence stands out as conspicuously as that of missing teeth.

No matter how keen one's sight may be, if his hearing is at fault he hunts under a perpetual handicap that robs him of bird after bird. My own, I realize, is not what it once was, and is rapidly getting no better. Under normal conditions I can still hear the first flutter of any bird that gets up within reasonable range, but the old ability to determine instantly the exact location of the sound, and to swing upon it unerringly with gun already coming into shooting position, has, I fear, gone from me forever.

Unless one has once had it, and lost it, it would be hard to imagine its real value. There are certain humans who do not possess it, and I am sure it is not so universally common among animals as one might suppose, for I have seen many a deer run directly toward the noise that alarmed it, and I know that but few of my dogs have ever been able to locate me readily by my whistle, for I have frequently watched them look all about in an effort to see me, even while I was making the forest echo with a piercing blast.

When one is forced to verify the evidence of his hearing by checking up on it with his eyesight, he loses that essential moment of time in which he formerly got the "jump" on the bird, for when one stands with gun at shoulder as he waits for his target to break into view, he has every advantage that the game affords. His mind is already leaping ahead, estimating the distance, checking up on the natural hazards which each shot presents, and making his lightning-like decision concerning the exact spot where he will make his bid for the quarry. But when the welcome flutter of wings leads him to believe the bird is breaking from the right or left to cross more or less diagonally before him, and he then catches a glimpse of it rocketing straight away, he not only finds himself off balance but he has the feeling that haste is imperative, and neither his position nor mental attitude is conducive of good shooting.

It is under conditions such as these that one may know how thoroughly he has learned his trade, and I derive no end of satisfaction from the thought that I know several gamy old chaps in their seventies who are still a very real menace to any grouse that flutters a wing in their immediate vicinity. I hope I may be similarly blessed, but I suppose that is asking more than I have a right to expect. Seventy still lies beyond many a hill, but it startles me sometimes to think how much nearer it seems than it did when I was thirty-five.

# CHAPTER V

I AM still old-fashioned enough to like babies, and to believe they play a rather important part in the present scheme of things. They are interesting and companionable, and at times display an almost human intelligence; but if there is anything else that is God-given and heaven-born, it is a genuine, honest-to-goodness grouse dog.

For thirty-five years of my life I entertained a different opinion. I knew that some dogs handled better than others, and seemed to have the luck to find more than their share of birds, but I supposed it was due to their training and experience, and such slight differences as there might be in the quality of their noses.

For no reason other than that of one or two painful experiences with an old and surly-tempered pointer, I championed the setter's cause, believing him to be more companionable, a trifle more capable, and considerably better fitted by nature to withstand the rough terrain and equally fearful weather conditions that a New England bird dog must forever face. I blush with shame because of my ignorance, and yet I realize it is often by such inconsequential things as these that our convictions are formed, for I know men who could not give one valid reason for their unshakable political faith.

Whenever in the course of those first hectic years I acquired a setter pup, my chief cause for worry was whether or not it would develop the pointing instinct. I remember how I used to haunt the woodlands, with a gangling long-legged puppy struggling along behind me, and how I would know nothing but hopeless despair when it failed to be excited by the scent left by a departing bird. What joy was mine when after months of waiting I saw it suddenly freeze into immobility as some newly discovered scent tingled in its nostrils! I did not know the chances were less than one in a thousand that it would not eventually do so, and I was thrilled by the thought that here was a potential bird dog who, with proper training, could hold its own with the best of its kind.

I don't know why I should have been so foolish. I knew that *Lou Dillon* could trot faster than any other horse in the world. I knew that Fitzsimmons had experienced some difficulty in extracting his glove from Corbett's stomach. I knew that Cy Young had a trifle more of what the present generation would designate as "smoke" on the ball than any of his fellows, and yet it never occurred to me that all dogs did not possess the same natural ability.

It happened years ago, but my face still burns when I recall a mistake I made while I was still struggling through those formative years, and from which I did not profit until long, long afterward. The sound of an occasional shot in a strip of woods adjacent to that where I was hunting, drew me over to see who was encroaching on a domain to which I could not help but feel I had prior rights.

Coming into it presently, and hearing the distant crackle of brush, I hurried on and soon encountered a white-haired, bespectacled Nimrod, whom I immediately recognized as a market hunter from an adjoining town. He answered my salutation civilly enough, but was not as enthusiastic over the meeting as I had hoped he would be, nor did he recognize me as a fellow member of the Great Fraternal Order of Grouse Exterminators. He was even less enthusiastic when, a few moments later, he discovered that I was trailing along behind him.

"Is that gun loaded, Sonny?" he asked, turning upon me suddenly.

A foolish question I thought, inasmuch as I was bird hunting, but I answered that it was.

"Then please don't keep the thing pointed at my back."

A pessimistic sort of chap he seemed, and not too companionable, but I magnanimously decided to overlook his faults for a time. My interest in him was already waning, but he was accompanied by a perfectly glorious white and ticked setter, and nothing short of physical violence could have altered my determination to see it do a bit of bird work.

With the muzzle of my gun carefully lowered, I plodded along in the path he made, and was presently rewarded by seeing the dog go cautiously forward and then come to an abrupt halt. Its master went in confidently, but he was still some thirty feet from it when the dog relaxed a trifle, moving ahead and to the right for a distance of fifty feet or more before again coming to a halt.

It was not much of a dog after all, I thought, and my suspicion was confirmed when, before we had covered half the distance that now separated us, it moved on again, walking slowly and cautiously, as though it were treading on eggs.

My companion's movements were decidedly unorthodox, too, for instead of following behind his dog until such time as it had arrived at a decision whether to point or not, he struck off by a circuitous route that would carry him to a point well ahead of the evidently perplexed animal, and traveled off at a pace I found it difficult to follow.

That his maneuver was well planned was proven shortly thereafter, for as he swung down into the approximate path the dog would presently tread, a grouse burst out before him. He gathered it in neatly, the dog came in and retrieved it, and received a friendly pat on the head as a reward.

"Nice work, old boy," the stranger said, as he stuffed the bird into his already bulging coat. "Well, good-bye, Sonny. I'll see you again sometime—I suppose."

I had seen enough to satisfy me, but I resented the tone he employed, and I struck where I knew the blow would hurt.

"It took him quite a while to locate that bird, didn't it?" I said, and made it sound more like an authoritative statement than a question.

"What do you mean, locate it?" he asked, and never have I heard contempt more fully expressed in seven syllables.

"Why," I replied, "He was five minutes in finding it."

That look he gave me as he turned and walked away! No words could have conveyed half its meaning, and I had never been so conscious of my youth and inexperience. I was fully aware that I was a gibbering idiot, but for the life of me, and for many years thereafter, I could not guess how he happened to determine the fact so readily.

Eight or ten years rolled past before I saw another dog road a running bird in like manner, and not until it was over did I understand why that old pot hunter of long ago had looked at me as he did. An elderly friend—who possessed only an infinitesimal part of my enthusiasm for grouse, but many times my financial ability to gratify it—bought a three-year-old setter that was broken on quail, but was not fast or rangy enough for the work.

The description sounded interesting, for I was beginning to suspect that a dog needed something more than winged feet to cope successfully with partridge, and it was upon my advice that he made the purchase. Since then I have seen one dog, and one only, that was better than he, and I think the cause for that was because during the first three years of his life the grouse population reached one of the highest peaks I have ever known; but I learned more from his predecessor concerning the things a genuine grouse dog can do than I have ever learned from another of his kind. Grouse attracted him as water attracts ducks, and he took to them as naturally. His physical limitations, and his inborn reluctance to get out and travel at a speed which rendered it impossible for him to touch anything but a few of the high spots, made his range perfectly adapted to our covers, and he was possessed of an intelligence of a high order. I doubt if he had ever scented a grouse until I took him out, but from the first day there was no question in my mind that he was something different in the way of a bird dog than anything I had previously handled.

Well do I remember our second trip with him. Lying a little apart from the section of woods we intended to hunt, was a long, narrow run between two steep banks, covered with alders and stunted gray birches for its entire quarter-mile length.

We had no more than entered the tangle at the lower end when the dog pointed momentarily, then loosened up and went cautiously ahead for a few steps before halting again. Telling my companion to keep well up on the bank and far enough ahead to enable him to get a shot at the bird when it got up, I waited until he had gained his position and then started toward the dog. I was still some distance behind him when he moved ahead once more, but now his attitude had changed. So far as the use of them was concerned, there might as well not have been a joint in his legs from his body down, for they were as stiff as iron rods, and he moved forward upon them after the manner of a boy walking on stilts.

Some glimmer of reason told me that he was pointing as solidly as dog ever pointed, even while he moved ahead, and the memory of that other setter I had seen trail a running bird came back to me in an illuminating flash. I called guardedly to the watcher on the bank to keep moving ahead, and followed along in the rear of the procession.

For ten minutes thereafter, I witnessed a display of bird work that was a revelation to me. I knew that grouse frequently ran before a dog, for I had seen them stealing silently away through the shadows. Many a time I had seen a dog freeze into a sudden and intense point, only to loosen up again a few moments later and look around in confusion before he rushed ahead either to find the scent again or to send the bird thundering away before him; but this fellow followed his quarry step by step, pausing momentarily as the bird paused, often even shrinking back a trifle as some unexplained sense warned him that it was becoming unduly alarmed, then going ahead once more, with head held high and nose outthrust before him, and moving ever a little from side to side that he might be in the exact center of the invisible thread which linked him so securely to the bird.

The cover, as I have said, was at least a quarter of a mile in length, but he went to within fifty feet of its upper end before he again came to a rigid halt. There was nothing left for the bird to do except to expose himself by taking to the air, or attempt to circle and steal back along its former course. As I stood there, wondering what decision it would make, I saw the dog's head begin to turn slowly—slowly— toward the left, and I knew the bird had chosen the latter plan.

The alders were shorter there, and I could readily see above them. Telling my companion to get ready, I left the dog and cut back to head the bird. It came out with a grand commotion, and headed for the watcher on the bank. He ducked to give it plenty of room to pass, then turned and centered it with a charge from his full-choke gun at a distance of less than thirty feet. Feathers flew, like the first awesome blast of ashes from an erupting volcano, as the bird paid for its indiscretion to the last, full measure; and my companion raised his voice in melancholy lament because the floating feathers were about all that was left of the once-proud bird; but my heart was singing a paean of exultation. After more than fifteen years of blind groping for something which I had not been at all sure existed, I had at last found a grouse dog.

It changed my whole perspective of hunting. Hitherto no day had been complete unless its close found me with a reasonably full game bag. It was not to be wondered at, for I had been reared in the oldtime atmosphere that had prevailed in this country since the days of the Pilgrim Fathers, and had thought that the winning of the game was more to one's credit than the manner in which it was played.

That it is time for an oldtimer to accept the modern point of view I know from my own experience and other proofs which I have gleaned from time to time. Very recently a grizzled old fellow recounted for my benefit the diabolical machinations of a perverse fate that had turned what might have been a perfectly glorious day into one that would go down in history as the most deplorable in his experience.

He had started out that morning with the hope that he might be so fortunate as to bring down his legal limit of one deer, and was somewhat surprised when, in less than an hour's time, he bagged a fine buck.

So far, he had no quarrel with fate, but it was not long before his ill fortune began. Leaning his rifle against a tree, he had no more than started to disembowel his prize when has attention was attracted by the sound of a stamping hoof, and he looked up into the eyes of a truly gigantic doe that stood watching him from a distance of less than fifty yards.

It was then that his ill fortune began, for at his first movement toward the rifle the doe bounded away, and although he did manage to release one shot as she vanished from view, the bullet perversely went astray. The disappointment was enough to make a strong man weep, but the end was not yet, for while he was dragging out his prize—with his rifle unloaded for safety's sake—another buck bounded out into an opening before him and got cleanly away.

That was the basis of his quarrel with the Goddess of Luck. If she had just stayed away and minded her own business he might have had five hundred pounds of meat instead of the measly one hundred and seventy pounds he did get.

I regret that some men still play the game so unfairly,

but I am glad that so many of them, and especially the younger generation, are learning, as I learned that day behind the trailing dog, to play the game for its own sake.

That setter had an affinity for grouse that was truly remarkable. There was a sureness about his every movement, even from the first, that I have seen equaled in only one other of his kind. He traveled with an effortless, pacing motion that was as smooth as the flight of a swallow, and although he had been urged to get out on the horizon, we had not hunted him a week before he was ranging at a pace exactly suited to our heavy covers, and it had required only a few suggestions on my part to get him to do so.

Out of every ten thousand children there is one who can begin the study of a violin, and in a year's time learn to play it better than could all the rest in a long, long lifetime. I think real grouse dogs are similarly blessed at birth, and I am not at all certain they occur in a greater proportion than do real violinists.

Without any previous training on them, this setter came up from the southland and set about handling grouse like an old master. At first he occasionally flushed a bird, but the season was not half ended when we could go for days without hearing one take wing because of any fault of his. He had, too, an uncanny instinct or foreknowledge of the manner in which individual birds would act at his approach, for he would go in boldly upon one and freeze into a sure and convincing point that said as plainly as words, "You can come right in and pry this one loose, Sir. He's nailed to the ground," while he might approach the next with the most infinite caution and then crouch and creep forward for the last few feet, and he was almost invariably right in his judgment. When he said, "This is a jittery one, Sir! For goodness' sake, be careful!" it behooved one to watch where he placed his feet, and to set himself for instant action.

Neither before nor since have I seen a dog so infallibly accurate in locating his birds. I suppose it was because of the fine judgment he had concerning the last inch of distance he could safely make toward them that he was able to designate their positions so precisely, but whatever the cause, the bird was always where he said it was. Dozens of times I have seen him slide to an abrupt stop as a new and hot scent came to his nostrils, and then so slowly that one had to watch it intently to discern the movement, turn his head to the right or left, and when it came to rest his nose was pointing at the bird.

It was he who solved, to my satisfaction at least, a mystery that had bothered me for a long time. Ever since I could remember, I had heard the oft-recurring phrase, "They'll lie to this dog." At first I did not know what it meant, but gradually I came to understand that those who uttered it believed that some dogs possessed an occult charm so powerful that its influence could be felt by the bird: a sort of long range hypnotism that robbed it of its power of flight, and caused it to forget all its caution and inborn cunning.

I doubt if among all the whims and fancies concerning grouse there is a more erroneous belief. I have shot over a number of dogs whose performance might easily have given rise to the theory, for what even their owners did not seem to realize was the fact that the close-lying, bold birds were the only ones on which the dogs were able to get points. Those that stole softly away were quite frequently the cause of false points which the owners quite rightly explained by saying, "There's been game of some kind around here," and those the dogs put up by an incautious approach were anathematized and branded as, "The wildest I've ever seen"; but when one of them chose valor rather than discretion for its motto, they firmly believed it was some baleful influence exuding from the dog that held it there.

Later, as I have said, it was my privilege to hunt for seven seasons over an even better dog than the one who had taught me that all grouse could be handled. I do not think he had any more brains than the other whose son he was, or any more bird-sense, but he had the best nose I have ever known a bird dog to possess, and he had infinitely better opportunities to use it.

The fact that his master was offered five hundred dollars for him should prove something of his worth, and the fact that the fellow got away with a whole skin should also prove something of the self-control the owner was able to exercise; but only by hunting behind him for a few days could one even begin to estimate his true worth.

His first year in the woods was at the beginning of the last upward swing of birds that brought them back to anywhere near their oldtime numbers, and he had more of them killed over him than many present-day dogs will ever be privileged to smell. The season limit at that time was fifty birds, and year after year his owner and I each took that number in two states, and innumerable woodcock and Wilson snipe in addition.

It was no wonder he was good, for not only was he a once-in-a-lifetime dog, but he had the opportunity to perfect his exceptional qualities until his performance was flawless. I realize that it sounds incredible, but I have hunted behind him for many days in succession without once putting up a bird that he was neither pointing nor trailing. He did the latter as his father had done before him, never sniffing the ground, but with head held high in the air, and nostrils widely expanded, followed his bird as readily and as surely as though he could see its every movement.

The distance at which he could scent grouse was amazing. Hundreds of times I have seen him stop and thrust his head high in the air for a moment, then turn and start steadily off—at a pace he soon learned to adjust to ours—in a bee-line for a spot I sometimes fancied we would never reach, but when he had run that thread of scent down to its source there was always a grouse at the end of it.

From the first, he was permitted to break shot in order to retrieve. My personal opinion is that it is a bad practice, yet after he had hunted two seasons I doubt if there was ever a year when he put up more than one or two birds by so doing.

It was because of him that I formed some ideas concerning quartering which still persist, even though at times they meet with quite strenuous opposition. Theoretically a dog is supposed to cover all the ground if he expects to find all the birds. The argument is sound and entirely logical. It is quite possible that a dog who ranges according to his best judgment rather than by a blueprint will occasionally pass one up in some out-of-the-way corner, but I'll venture to say that the chap who follows along and depends for his daily sustenance upon the birds which a good dog leaves behind will occasionally go to bed without satisfying all the cravings of the inner man.

In all my life I have seen but two dogs who quartered systematically, and, by a strange coincidence, I would not have accepted either of them as a gift. The first was a Gordon setter, as beautiful a specimen of his kind as I have ever seen, but although his angles were geometrically correct as he worked back and forth before his master, he would not range out more than thirty feet, even in the most open country. I liked him very much, for he was a companionable fellow, but at the end of a day's hunt behind him I always felt that we would have found an almost equal number of birds without him.

The other was a female pointer, a wonder dog whose praises I had heard sung for a year or two, and one that I drove many miles to see. I doubt if any man ever owned a gamier-acting dog, or one in whom the desire to hunt was more firmly implanted, but she was the most glaring example of overtraining I have ever seen. More than anything else in the world she reminded me of an unfortunate and weak-willed woman who had been so browbeaten and overridden by a hulking brute of a husband that she no longer dared call her soul her own.

I hunted behind the dog for several hours, and not once in all that time did I see her do a wrong thing. She turned on a dime at his whistle, went where he sent her, and hunted her ground thoroughly and well; but not one move did she make until she was sure it would meet with her trainer's approval, and ninety per cent of her attention was given to him, rather than to the important task of finding birds.

Those moments when she winded game were a nightmare to me, and I am sure they were to her also, for if ever a dog needs the assurance and self-reliance that comes from a consciousness of its ability to cope with the situation unassisted, it needs it then. She went in fearfully, the memory of the unpleasant aftermaths of a hundred similar situations uppermost in her mind, looking backward occasionally and keeping her ears cocked for an expected command.

I was glad when it was over, for it still stands out as one of the most unpleasant days in my experience, and it was not brightened at any time by the thought of the moment of parting. The fellow had a dominating personality that even I could feel, and my state of mind was comparable to that of the dog as I worried over what answer I would make to his inevitable question, "Well, what do you think of her?" I abhor dissimulation, preferring to be direct rather than diplomatic, but I just couldn't follow my natural inclination. I told him, instead, that he had the most thoroughly trained dog I had ever seen, and bade him goodbye.

Let it not be inferred, though, that I am not in favor of teaching a dog to quarter his ground with at least some degree of system. Even among the so-called "good" dogs I think it would produce more points than a haphazard and slipshod method, but I believe there is an occasional one born with such a nose and brain and natural grouse-ability that he can work out a system of his own which will not only be equally productive but will conserve his strength as well.

Probably every bird hunter will admit that his dog's efficiency is considerably less when it becomes tired, and most of them are aware that three or four hard days' hunting each week are all that even a well-conditioned dog can stand. My present dog is a three-year-old pointer, lean and muscular, and exercised daily, yet he hunts so fast and furiously that he would need a set of crutches on which to hobble before the third successive day had ended.

His assets, as I list them, are a glorious disposition, an average nose, a rock-like staunchness, and boundless enthusiasm. On the other side of the ledger I must write that when the scent of running grouse grows faint in his nostrils, he stands with a blank and baffled look on his face, and cannot think of a single thing he can do about it. He shows a marked preference for woodcock, and he has not the reasoning power to grasp the fact that if he used his nose more and his feet less he might accompany me every day instead of alternate ones.

[ 180 ]

That bit of knowledge was something which the glorious setter of whom I spoke, worked out for himself and used thereafter to good advantage. For the seven active years of his life he hunted through every suitable day of the two months' season, and could have done twice as much with equal ease. After the natural exuberance engendered by the excitement of the first few days had worn off, he would settle down to a plan he had designed to keep production at its highest point and labor down to a minimum.

He always worked as far in advance as the cover would permit him to do and still be in direct contact with us, keeping always well down on the windward side and quartering his ground not at all. It was as unorthodox a proceeding as a bird hunter could imagine, but on several occasions I have seen some of them bow their heads humbly because they ventured to suggest that their Jack or Sport or Pard could find a like number of birds—and a dozen more that we had missed as we went along. The setter's owner had but one answer for that, for he had a sublime and rightful confidence in his dog. "There is only one way to determine that," he would say. "Bring him along tomorrow and let him prove it."

Some of them accepted the challenge and some did not, but only the latter were privileged to retain their original opinion. The presence of another dog bothered the setter not at all, for he drifted serenely and quietly along his way, unfretting and unhurried, but ever and anon lifting his head high in the air and striking obliquely off on an unseen trail that led directly to a bird. Hunting against the best dog ever put down beside him, he found, in three successive days, exactly five grouse to each of his rival's one. On another never-to-be-forgotten day, against a dog whose owner's voice had been raised the loudest in condemnation, he gave us twenty-seven productive points on grouse, and his brace mate gained nothing but an occasional opportunity to back, and a lesson in good manners which I imagine lingered long in his memory.

The wily setter had gone nonchalantly along, nailing birds to left and right to the utter bewilderment of his companion, who either backed him half-heartedly or not at all. I could tell the boastful owner's ire was rising at each successive defeat, and I imagine his feelings were in some way communicated to his dog, for quite suddenly it decided to distinguish itself, for once at least. The setter had angled off to freeze solidly on another bird that chanced to lie in an open glade where we could plainly watch the little drama unfold. The pointer spied him almost as soon as he paused, and leaving his own fruitless quest, bounded over, came up beside him, sniffed hungrily for the briefest of moments, and then started to crowd past.

[ 182 ]

He received the surprise of his life—and so did I, for while the setter was one of the gentlest and most companionable animals I had ever known, he grabbed the discourteous fellow by the back of the neck, and, if I may be permitted to use the phrase, shook the everlasting daylight out of him.

For a few moments the neighboring forest echoed to their clamor, but it was over shortly. The pointer went whimpering back where he belonged—and the setter went ahead two steps and took up his job where he had temporarily abandoned it, for strange though it may sound, the grouse, throughout all that turmoil and strife had remained firmly rooted beneath a protecting juniper bush.

Partly because our twenty years of friendship gives him the right to do so, and partly because our ideas about grouse dogs differ widely, an oldtime shooting partner of mine is at once my most constructive and severe critic. In all things concerning fishing we are tuned to the same key, but such harmony as we achieve when dogs are our theme is, I fear, of the barbershop variety.

I believe the power to locate and trace scent to be many times greater in some dogs than in others; he thinks that barring sickness or accident, all are equally blessed. I believe physical stamina varies as much in dogs as it does in humans; he insists it is wholly a matter of diet and exercise.

I believe a super grouse-dog must be born with something special in the way of bird sense; he says it is entirely a matter of environment and education. I think I have learned something about their training; he insists I couldn't teach one to use a sawdust box. Concerning them we are of a united opinion in only one thing. Each of us believes himself to be right.

To me it would sound fully as silly to assert that all members of the human race are equally endowed at birth with mental and physical characteristics. The fact that my friend and I entertain conflicting opinions is proof enough that our reasoning processes differ, and I know, as surely as I know anything, that dogs are as dissimilar as we.

Science has not yet been able to prove how a foxhound can take one sniff at a track in the snow and then start off upon it in the right direction. I could never determine how my dog can distinguish between my tracks and those of my hunting companion when our rubber footwear is made by the same company, yet some of them have been able to do it remarkably well.

A Montagnais Indian trapper in Quebec told me a story that sounds wholly incredible, and yet I hesitate to say it was not the absolute truth.

Like the rest of the tribe, he was dependent upon fur for his daily bread, and when wire noose and steel trap failed

to procure it, he used poison baits. In order to reap the re-
wards accruing from this nefarious practice it was necessary
to have a dog that would trail the victims, and never have
I seen a more disreputable looking specimen than the one
whose praises he sung. All its original identifying characteristics had been lost in a thousand miscellaneous matings,
and the result was a typical "Indian dog"; but his eyes were
so widely spaced that there was a handbreadth between
them, and they were bright with intelligence.

At first his master regaled me with stories of the dog's
prowess in following the maddened wanderings of the poi-
soned animals, and then, because I believed him, he explained how thoroughly it had learned to avoid even the
most cunningly concealed trap or snare. I could swallow
that readily enough, too, for I had seen bird dogs who
would back warily away from a heap of freshly turned sand
at the edge of a juniper bush, after they had once or twice
had their toes pinched because of their curiosity.

Then he said, in the best English I had heard for many
a day, "These things we can believe, because we can understand them, but I could tell you other things which you
would doubt. I doubt it sometimes, because my head tells
me no, even though I have seen it and know it is the truth."

He told me then, how, although a foot of snow might
lie upon the ice, the dog would follow along above an otter

that was swimming beneath it, and recounted several experiences in which he had captured the animal by stamping along behind the dog and driving the suffocating otter away from the life-giving bubbles of its exhaled breath.

It seems wholly incredible—but scarcely more so than to see a bird dog nail a grouse that sits some fifty or sixty feet above him in the very top of a high, old pine; yet I have seen the latter thing done so often that it has ceased to impress me as being an unusual occurrence.

The point, then, at which I have been so long in arriving, is that there is a big and fruitful field for someone who will devote his life to developing a strain of dogs whose forte is the handling of ruffed grouse. We have bred them for almost every other conceivable purpose, from the baiting of bulls, down to the smug-faced and snobbish little watch-charm editions, whose sole mission in life is to enhance milady's charm; but apparently nobody has seriously tried to perfect a type especially adapted to grouse hunting.

I think that most oldtimers will agree that birds are far harder to handle than they were no longer than twenty-five years ago. It is not that they are wilder, but I think they better understand the nature of the danger and have worked out a plan to defeat it. I am referring, of course, to the hard-hunted and educated birds. Those of the big woods, to whom man remains an unknown quantity, are still the fool hens they always were, but it goes without saying that those who encounter hunters almost daily throughout the hunting season, and still survive, have devised a workable solution to the problem of existence.

A great many more now try to steal quietly away than did formerly, and when they do decide to fly, they often go twice their oldtime distance. I can remember when we used to make it a point to mark down all survivors when a flock got up before us, then go look them up one by one, and find them within fifty yards of where we thought they were. But as a rule, the fellow who tries it now is only wasting his time. There used to be a saying that until an hour before sunset, one should look for his grouse upon the ground, but after then the majority of flushed birds would take to trees. Like any rule, there were occasional exceptions, but it was reasonably dependable, and I killed many a grouse by looking up rather than down as the day was drawing to a close.

No longer, however, does the saying hold true. Only last fall, and in the middle of the day, I repeatedly saw grouse flush wild, and listening intently, I heard them alight in distant pines. In the old days it was a common occurrence to have young and unsophisticated birds hop up among the low limbs at the approach of a dog, and sit there brainlessly as we picked them off one by one, but these were actuated by reason rather than its lack. They got up at a distance, and flew fast and far; and they went into the tree-tops because they knew that with a man and a dog after them, they were far safer there than on the ground.

The bird that lies closely now is the exception rather than the rule, and unless a dog is a specialist in handling that type of wily old running rascal he will look foolish a greater part of the time.

I regret that I did not have the foresight to acquire that first superlative setter, or at least to buy a pair of his off-spring, but I did not, and with the exception of one of his sons I have never had the opportunity to see another of his kind. Undoubtedly they exist, and undoubtedly they are ridiculed to scorn by all field-trial men, but the fellow who owns one has a potential gold mine if he can hit upon a mating that will produce others like him.

I realize how greatly opinions vary, and I am painfully aware of the worthlessness of most of mine, but I would like to record some of the virtues a grouse dog must have in order to satisfy me. It is hard to set them down in the order of their importance, for all are essential, and each is dependent upon the other to make a perfect whole. After due deliberation, I think I shall list intelligence as the first requisite, although in doing so I wish to make a sharp distinction between that commodity and mere knowledge, and I can best illustrate my meaning by citing the case of George.

George's father was an uncouth and uneducated back-woodsman whom I knew in my youth, but he had an inherited Yankee shrewdness and a business acumen which enabled him to amass a sizable fortune in the lumber industry. Realizing the handicap he had always been forced to combat, he decided that son George should not be similarly burdened, and sent him to a good prep school, and afterward to college.

When his son returned with his cap and sheepskin, the old man heaved a sigh of vast relief, and settled comfortably back to let George carry on the business; but somehow it didn't work out as he had planned. He was back in the harness again in less than a month, and George had departed to the city, where he had accepted a "position."

Confiding his woes to a sympathetic listener, the old man epitomized an all-too-common failing.

"George has got book larnin' enough," he said, "but the trouble with the durn cutter is he don't *know* anything."

My dream dog may be uneducated, but he must have a capacity for knowledge, and he must be capable of working out all his greater problems for himself. No matter how skilled a trainer I may be, the things which lie within my power to teach him are not fundamentals but merely frills, and the influence they have upon his bird work are at best only negligible. I can, and should, influence him to hunt to gun. If we are both headstrong and determined each to have his own way, I have the power to force him to do as I wish; but if after I have killed birds over him for a few weeks he cannot figure out the reason why he should keep in close touch with me, he will find it hard work to qualify as a top-notch grouse dog.

I can teach him staunchness. Without too much trouble I can cause him to stop at my command and not move an inch until I give the word—but if he does not come shamefacedly back to me when he accidentally flushes a bird, there is something wrong which no teaching of mine can correct.

I can help him at first to follow a moving bird. When he loses it, and hurries foolishly about, I can encourage him to move on in what I judge to be the right direction—but if he hasn't the brains to put his nose in the air and run that thread of scent down to its source, I can do nothing about it. He must be gifted with other things as well, but if he hasn't the intelligence to use them he is hopeless.

Second in the matter of importance, I would list what dog men term "nose," for no matter how bounteously he may be blessed with brains, a dog is helpless unless his scenting powers are of the choke-bore type. It is not enough for him merely to become aware that a bird lurks somewhere in his immediate vicinity, but he must know its location as surely as though he could see it; and in saying so, I am not considering the hunter's point of view.

Most dogs will point well under favorable conditions, but the thing which distinguishes the top-notcher from the other kind is his ability to determine the exact spot from which the scent comes. Without that ability, even a cautious dog will flush his birds far too often, and he will be unable to trail the moving ones by body scent alone, which he must do if he hopes to be successful. The dog that puts its nose to the ground and trails by foot scent, in the majority of instances is beaten from the start.

So long as the bird travels in a straight line, the dog has a chance, but the moment it moves to one side or doubles back upon its course the chance is all too great that the dog will blunder upon it, and another bird is added to the list of those who refused to lie for the dog.

Then, too, the hunter is tremendously handicapped while shooting over a dog that cannot accurately locate scent, for he has no opportunity to use his judgment, but must depend upon blind chance to give him a reasonably clear and close shot. Under the best of conditions he will all too frequently make mistakes, but the satisfaction of occasionally being right will more than outweigh the chagrin arising from his errors.

Lastly, although not in the order of its importance, I

would place grouse-sense as one of the cardinal requirements. With a keen brain, a supersensitive nose and inborn
grouse-sense, any dog has the essentials from which cham-
pions are made. The first two are often encountered, although not together so frequently as one might suppose,
but the chance of finding all three in one animal is considerably less than that of drawing a royal flush in a poker
game. It has happened, and will again, but so long as it is
contingent upon blind chance it will never occur with any
degree of frequency.

The requirements for a woodcock dog are not so exact-
ing, for the little russet chap is far easier to handle; but here,
too, a keen nose is of the utmost importance. It always
seemed to me that the infinite caution which characterizes
a high-class grouse dog works to his disadvantage while
hunting the smaller and more closely lying bird. On widely
scattered singles, or on the occasional one encountered in
grouse country, those two good dogs I mentioned would
nail their birds as accurately and quickly as anyone could
wish, but in a white-splashed and highly scented concentration area during a heavy flight, they would creep cautiously about, fearfully expecting that each step would send
a woodcock skittering into the air, while a dog that couldn't
hold a candle with them on grouse would flash boldly about
and nail one after another with uncanny precision.

I love to hunt woodcock, and I know of no other bird so perfectly adapted to the hunter's need for something on which to work his young dog, but nevertheless if I were starting a promising youngster, and intended to do everything in my power to make him the best possible grouse dog, I would teach him that woodcock were to be classed with rabbits, and that both were definitely scratched off our list.

So much has been written about dog training that one would need to be another Solomon to add to the store of accumulated knowledge, but I have yet to read a writer who has clearly defined the status which should exist between man and dog. Here, too, conditions vary, and what might be accepted as gospel by one would be regarded as rank heresy by another. My personal preference is for the old boy-and-dog intimacy, but the chap who is forced to board his dog at a kennel for ten months of the year can hardly expect to be so blessed.

The "Man the master, and dog the abject slave" attitude is an ideal one—if the dog voluntarily places himself in that position. When he lies at your feet for hours, with an "Oh, Sir, you are wonderful," look in his eyes, you may not rank highly as a dog trainer, but you may rest assured you are on the right track.

I recall seeing an old series of humorous cartoons that

portrayed the similarity between men and their dogs, and while the artist let his imagination have full sway, there was a great basic truth in his idea, for dogs do most certainly take on some of the characteristics of their masters.

No other animal is so quick to sense human emotions, and no other is so easily influenced by them. If you lose your temper while putting the youngster through a period of his daily schooling, you may be quite certain that it will work out to your disadvantage, and if you get flustered and excited when birds begin to go up all around you, it is a safe bet that the dog will be excited also.

I have heard men say, "The more I knock my dog around the better he likes me," but I doubt if Ananias ever thought of a better one than that. Quite likely the dog will try to establish the old friendly relations, but I doubt if his love is appreciably greater than it was before, and I am sure the man has risen neither in his own respect nor mine. While most young dogs need to be corrected at times, yet even our strait-laced Plymouth ancestors learned after a time that tying an erring brother to a whipping post and administering nine lashes with a knotted "cat," was not an infallible cure for all the weaknesses of the flesh.

My boyhood spaniel chum discovered quite early in life that killing chickens could be a fascinating sport, and because our nearest neighbor was some distance away, he confined his activities of that sort to members of our own flock. The consensus of opinion was that I was far too young to know anything about dog training, so Dad took the culprit out to the chicken run, whipped him smartly and drove him back to the house.

The next day he killed *two* chickens. Now, Dad was a conscientious seeker after truth, so he harnessed the horse and we drove several miles to the home of a self-appointed veterinarian, who was reputed to know the answers to all questions pertaining to dogs. He recommended as the one sure cure, that we tie a dead chicken to the pup's collar, and leave it there as an odoriferous reminder of his misdemeanor. I was opposed to the procedure, but I was a very small minority, and the plan was put into practice.

That night the pup chewed off all but the dangling legs, and evidently finding the taste to his liking, went out the next day and indulged in a perfect orgy of fowl play, leaving the ground strewn with feathers and mortal remains.

It chanced that shortly after the carnage had ended the minister came to call. A kindly old soul he was, revered and respected by all who knew him, and looked upon as one in whom was vested all the wisdom of the ages. Naturally, he was called upon for advice, and I shall never forget how solemnly I awaited his decision, for I was aware that these depredations must cease or I lose my black-and-white pup.

The elder touched learnedly upon all the forces that were at play in the dog's nature. He explained how centuries of selective breeding had inculcated in the animal a lust for feathers which only physical contact could satiate, and he made a fine point of the fact that we also were imbued with original sin. Lastly, he expressed the opinion that the pup could never be cured of the vicious habit.

When he had taken his departure, I listened to an ultimatum. The dog would have to be broken at once—or else.

That put the matter directly up to me. I didn't know the least thing about training dogs, but I took mine in my arms, carried him out into the chicken run, and, still holding him, sat down on the grass beneath an apple tree. After a time a chicken came up and looked us over inquisitively. The pup quivered, and struggled to break away, but I held him and told him "No!" Other chickens came up and the scene was reënacted, although I thought his struggles were a trifle less violent. Presently they ceased altogether, whereupon we got up and walked about among the chickens— and from that moment they were as safe in his company as though he were their foster parent. I didn't know a thing about dogs, and therefore I was obliged to fall back upon common sense.

I fear the most of us use too little of it in bringing up our pups and our children, for while there is a great similarity between them, no hard and fast rule will apply even to several individuals in one family. Each has a different temperament, and each must be regarded as a new problem and dealt with accordingly.

Although a great many cynics will doubt my word, I know a few children who respect their parents, and obey them because they love them. I know a still smaller group who occasionally act like the offspring of human beings because they fear the consequences if they do otherwise, but only in the first do I see any hope for the betterment of civilization. I am old-fashioned enough to prefer the latter to the great majority who know no other restraint than that imposed by a lethargic John Law, but I submit that the first group is in better control, whether they are under direct parental supervision or away from it.

The ideal status between dog and man should be of a similar nature. I am acquainted with several professional trainers who are good men. They know dogs far better than I. They are conscientious in their work, they use good judgment, and turn out a finished product—but not one of them can train a dog for my personal use as well as I can do it myself.

The reason is the very human one of which every workman is aware. He resents taking orders from anyone but his boss, and that dogs share the feeling is proven by the fact that mine will not obey any of my shooting companions as cheerfully as he minds me.

Although the two outstanding grouse dogs I have known were setters, I am broad-minded enough to confess that I believe the fact proves absolutely nothing. The only means we have of comparing the breeds is by their field-trial work, and so far as grouse hunting is concerned, even the winning of a championship is a poor measuring-stick by which to judge.

Neither should the opinion of experts influence us unduly, for it is obvious if they were not prejudiced in favor of one breed they would be handling the other kind. The one thing on which most of them agree, is that the pointer can be campaigned at an earlier age. Some high-strung quality in the setter's make-up renders it difficult to handle him as a derby prospect, and that fact alone may account for a part of the overwhelming majority of pointers entered in every event.

In bird-finding ability, many great trainers rank the two breeds as equal, and a few give the edge, if any, to the setter. From this it would seem that the pointer might gain the advantage of at least one season's hunting before the setter started, but again individual characteristics vary, and one may only generalize, and think in terms of percentages.

I owned one female setter that hunted and pointed

grouse quite consistently before she was six months old—
and the pointer I now have was seventeen months of age
before he showed any tendency to stand game. There was a
time when I believed the setter's coat would permit him to
hunt rougher country than the short haired breed, and I
fancied all the latter would go half a mile rather than wet
their feet; but one of my shooting companions has a pointer
that bores straight ahead through thorn bushes and brier
patches, and mine takes to even the iciest water as nonchalantly as a beaver.

Since there is so diversified an opinion, it is reasonable
to suppose that neither breed has any marked superiority
over the other as a shooting dog; and if I were buying one
tomorrow I wouldn't pay an extra penny where breed was
concerned. If I were selecting a pup I would be more interested in discovering signs of exceptional intelligence than I
would be in either size or conformation, although nobody
appreciates beauty in a dog more than I.

Were I choosing one that had been trained, I would try
to judge him on other things than the manner in which he
handled, although I would chalk it up in his favor if he
showed a willingness to accept suggestions. If he displayed
a tendency to fool with old scent, and showed by his manner
that he was bothered by it, I would keep on searching—but
in another direction. But if he put his nose in the air and

[ 199 ]

angled off upwind on a course that brought him directly to a grouse, and proved that he could repeat the performance, I would inquire his price—and would raise the money somehow.

These are my convictions. Some of them may be right, or they may all be wrong. I have not the omnipotent wisdom that was mine when I was twenty-one—or twice that, but if my opinion has no other merit, it is at least sincere.

# CHAPTER VI

I AM aware that a number of staid and conservative citizens in my community look upon me as a fit candidate for an asylum. They argue, and perhaps rightly, that any middle-aged man who spends two months of each year in chasing a bird dog around through the woods has something far more serious the matter with him than mere eccentricity.

In times past, before they learned to accept me as incurable, several of them tried to reason with me; and to the last man these self-appointed evangelists based their arguments on the financial loss I sustained by indulging my fancy. Their logic was unassailable because it was true, but they all shook their heads sadly and departed when they found I could not comprehend the fact that a bundle of green-tinted paper constituted wealth.

I am sane enough to realize that it is my attitude toward money that has prevented me from ever getting any of it, and I am human enough to wish I might have some of the things I have missed from life, but I have never been willing to purchase them at such a tremendous cost. Wealth, I have always thought, is an intangible asset, a spiritual condition based upon one's capacity for happiness and the amount of it he can crowd into his few short days.

For forty years I have known two men who have pursued happiness as zealously as I, although they have followed it along widely diverging trails. Which of them has been most successful I'll leave for you to decide.

"A" is a few years older than I. We once liked the same things. Quite frequently I encountered him in the woods or on a trout stream, but he always shot a clumsy old gun or fished with an alder pole. He could have owned better but he would not buy them, for already he had set his heart on the accumulation of money. Our ways parted when we reached manhood, and although I was never wholly out of touch with him, I was thirty years old when we were again thrown together. In the ten intervening years he had acquired a profitable business, and had charted all his plans for the future. He had not hunted or fished for years, nor would he for years to come, for his Plan would not permit it. His goal was money, and he was determined to push on toward it until he had accumulated exactly one hundred thousand dollars.

He topped the last hill in 1928, sold his business and retired, but the crash of 1929 took nearly half of his savings. He has the remainder yet, for he has never played. He forgot how during those hectic twenty years, and his spirit is now so broken that he can never again capture the magic thrill. Stooped, white-haired and old, he wanders about

with downcast eyes, and still believes the loss he has suffered can be computed in dollars and cents.

"B" and I are the same age. He loves the out-of-doors
as passionately as I, although he cares nothing for sports.
He is an amateur geologist, whose great ruling passion is
semi-precious stones, and he has been pursuing his hobby
for thirty years. His collection, although not famous, is a
creditable one. He is something of a lapidary, and during
the long winter evenings he cuts and polishes the best of his
season's collection. Their intrinsic value is slight, but they
are really beautiful; and he fusses with them and arrays
them in glass cases where they may catch and reflect the
light, and enjoys himself immensely.

I have never cited these examples to my critics. I dare
not, for I know what they would do. If they ever suspected
that I believed "B" to be the man who had amassed the
greater wealth, they would no longer look upon me as a
harmless simpleton, but would consider me a menace to
society, and try their best to have me committed.

"A" still has a portion of the money for which he slaved
so long, to give him what comfort he finds, and "B" has his
more tangible wealth of stones over which to gloat, but I
have stood alone on a western slope and watched the sun
sink down behind the purple hills. A small recompense,
some will say, for all the years that lie behind me, but my

imagination cannot conceive of the pile of money for which I would exchange my memories. Certainly not for "A's" stocks, nor yet for "B's" glittering treasures.

Memories! Gossamer things, of no more substance than dreams, yet how they come trooping back—and how priceless they are! I am glad I have lived long enough to gain a true perspective of myself in those early days, for some of my most joyous recollections are of events which were well-nigh tragic then.

I hope, for instance, that I may never forget the day when I stood on the station platform with Doc, or the moment when, after stamping up and down and swearing at the arctic wind that had robbed him of three more days of woodcock shooting, he stopped in his stride, snatched off the high-crowned broadcloth cap he wore, and turned down the concealed, beaver-skin ear muffs for greater protection against the biting blast.

It had been a fall of unseasonable cold, and an epidemic of something or other had robbed him of his customary week at Tracy's. When at last he had been able to get away, he had wished himself on me for a week. I liked him, but I was so young that I regarded him with awe rather than the admiration I should have accorded him, for his tongue was sharp as a whip lash, and he had a gruff, forbidding manner that deceived me for a time.

The heavy part of the flight was over, but a few belated stragglers kept dropping in, and they were sufficient for Doc's need. He blasted and blasphemed his way from cover to cover, shooting execrably, and calling down eternal disaster on the fate that had delayed him so long.

On the afternoon of the third day the skies thickened, the wind swung round into the north, and a driving sleet began to fall. It was the end of woodcock hunting for that season, and Doc again boiled over. He would, he asserted, take the first blank-blank train in the morning and go back to another blank-blank year of work.

Too disgruntled to more than nibble at the evening meal, he detailed me to tend his garments that were drying behind the kitchen stove, and retired to his room. Turning his shooting coat for the last time, I was about to follow his example, when I heard a ripping sound beneath the stove, and, looking down, I saw that my young setter had retrieved the illustrious headgear from where it had fallen, and holding it between her paws, had, with one fell motion, torn the beaver lining entirely out.

Thanks to the tanner's skill it had come out in one piece, and a hasty examination showed that nothing but the stitches had parted. With needle and thread I toiled far into the night, and when the job was finished I congratulated myself that my workmanship exceeded that of the maker,

[ 205 ]

for my stitches were fine and closely spaced, and not the tiniest hump stood up to mark the work of a tyro.

So there we stood on the platform, awaiting the frosty blast of a distant whistle—and Doc had turned down the ear muffs and clapped the cap back on his bald head, only to snatch it off again and glare down at it accusingly, while I broke out in a cold sweat because I had hesitated to tell him about it. Then he thrust it out for my inspection, and gave vent to all the disappointment he had suffered in one soul-stirring blast.

"Look at that!" he shouted, when he again became coherent. "The goddam fool who made it sewed that fur in wrong side out!"

A grand character, was Doc, and later I learned to appreciate him immensely, for his gruffness was but a screen he had erected to hide his real self, and his heart was as tender as a woman's. I am glad that his later years dealt kindly with him. As best he might, he had kept in touch with the game he loved to play, and when the time came when he could drop a part of his burden, he sprayed lead at woodcock from Nova Scotia to Cape Cod. He knew their ways and how to hunt them, and although his shooting never improved to a noticeable extent, I am sure he was utterly happy.

If ever a bird was cloaked in mystery, that bird is the

woodcock. Nocturnal in his habits, he is not only shy and secretive during the shooting season, but manages to keep his movements quite thoroughly concealed throughout the year. For many successive springs I have met him on his return from the southland, for it is then I like best to take pictures of my dogs; but although woodcock are reputed to nest very early in the season, I have never yet seen evidence of it, although one or two of my friends have found immature birds in early May.

Canoeing through Tobeatic Park in Nova Scotia last spring, I anticipated learning something of their nesting habits, for the southern part of the Province furnishes some of the best woodcock shooting in the world. Its broad, marshy areas are ideal nesting grounds for countless waterfowl, but although we saw young ducklings by the hundreds, and although each carry and every rock-strewn riffle through which we were forced to drag the canoe was spotted with splashings, I saw not one woodcock in the ten days I was there.

If one is familiar with its topography, or will but glance at a map, he can readily understand why Yarmouth County teems with them during the flight season, for all that southern tip is separated from the mainland by the Bay of Fundy, and birds trickle down from the interior to concentrate in the broad lowlands until they are driven by weather or migrating instinct to take off on their long flight to the coast.

I wonder why their departure has not been observed and fully described, for while it undoubtedly occurs at night, yet under conditions of early freezing temperatures or sudden snow storms it must be truly gigantic. It has been said that their flight often takes them as far as the Massachusetts coast, although I have never seen it officially verified. Quite likely the exodus is an individual rather than a group affair, with the consequent scattering of the birds over a large area, but even so, the numbers that sometimes move in a single night must be truly amazing.

It has always seemed to me that in Maine and New Hampshire at least, the southward flight of the birds conforms more or less with that of the coast line, in a broad band that stretches to the foothills, and that back of it they follow some of the larger river valleys. It would be interesting to know whether the northern birds follow the same route year after year, but I believe they do not, for I have known seasons when the Androscoggin Valley teemed with flight birds for weeks, while that of the Kennebec might have comparatively few, and the very next year the situation might be reversed. It proves nothing definitely, for an extreme drought, or any one of several conditions, might cut production to a minimum in one section of their breeding grounds and leave the remainder unimpaired. I hope

LYNN
BOGUE
HUNT

that sometime the Bureau of Biological Survey will find it practical to band a large number of birds in their breeding area, and then something definite may be learned concerning their flight through New England.

For a number of years, on the fifteenth of September, Bill and Herb and I used to start limbering up for the grouse season by loading a tent and all manner of miscellaneous supplies into an express wagon, hooking a plodding old horse into the shafts and striking off for a two-weeks' trip up the Saco or Androscoggin valleys after woodcock. It was a sort of Daniel Boone existence, for we traveled the unfrequented byways, and enjoyed all the thrills that any explorer knows.

In this day of fevered haste I imagine it is hard for the younger generation of sportsmen to picture those trips as they were, for where we crawled along over winding, single-track roads of live sand at a pace of three miles an hour, they can now travel at sixty, on a band of smooth and unyielding macadam. I am proud of the progress we have achieved as a nation of inventors, and I look forward with keen interest to the blessings which the future holds in store for mankind, but I deeply regret the loss of one thing which, I fear, is gone forever. I refer to the simple, unaffected and kindly hospitality one encountered everywhere. At the end of the first day's drive we were strangers in a strange land, but everyone we met tried to make us forget it and feel that we were welcome.

The thoughtlessness and wanton destruction displayed by the irresponsible horde who honk their riotous ways into every nook and corner of the land is the one great factor responsible for the change. No one sympathizes with the farmer and his problem of self-preservation more than I, for I still maintain an intimate contact with the soil, but I feel that I have lost something beyond price when instead of the cordial hail of good fellowship with which he used to greet me, I see one of them bearing belligerently down upon me with a pitchfork in his hand and a fighting look in his narrowed and jaundiced eyes.

I wish that it were possible to recapture for just one fall the happy and carefree attitude that was ours then, for we wandered about like gypsies, inquiring the whereabouts of hidden covers, and never once being refused every possible aid. We found some which are still productive, but many of them are now grown so old that the birds have long since deserted them, while others have been cut off and are now grown up again almost exactly as they were before.

There was a pleasing lonesomeness about the nights, too, and a feeling of isolation that somehow seems to have been beaten back by the advent of the automobile. All manner of big game roamed the forests at night, to wake us from our slumbers and cause us to grope stealthily for the smoke-blackened lantern and a sulphur match, or to steal quietly out into the moonlight, clad only in the briefest of shirts and a double-barreled shotgun, to stand shivering with cold and expectancy for long, long minutes while we waited for the intruder to show himself among the shadows.

I am sorry, too, for the smug attitude of mind that permits us to sleep so peacefully now after an evening spent around the campfire, when we have recounted all the weird and gruesome stories we have heard; for not the least of our joys then was the sudden start we experienced when an owl hooted from a nearby tree, or the tense wakefulness with which we lay huddled on our balsam beds and tried to find a rational explanation for some wholly unexplainable happening.

Well do I recall one such night. We had found a veritable paradise for woodcock, a large area of springy and rolling side-hills from which the timber pine had been stripped some years before. Young hardwood trees had sprung up, the windrows of brush had rotted down to conserve the natural moisture, and, finding it to their liking, a small army of northward-migrating birds had stopped there to nest.

For two days we had been doing our best to make them regret their decision, and we were entirely happy. We pitched our tent on a bit of rising ground that the old logging crew had once occupied, and cleaned out the bubbling spring from which they had quenched their thirst. The rough, board shacks which once housed them had long since been carted away, but a pole-studded and slab-shingled horse shed remained, old and weather-worn, but still water-tight and entirely serviceable.

In this building we stabled our horse, with a leather halter strapped firmly about his head, and the rope securely tied to a corner of the split-log feed rack. For protection against the cold night air, we closed the rusty-hinged plank door, and held it firmly shut by the simple expedient of propping an eight-foot log against it.

With the comforting assurance that the horse was warm and well fed, we slumbered serenely for two nights, but on the afternoon of the second day we encountered a native as we were making our way back to camp.

"Where are you fellers stoppin'?" he inquired, and we told him as best we could.

"An old horse shed, there, ain't they?" he asked.

We acknowledged the horse shed. He chewed meditatively for a few moments, staring at us thoughtfully, then spat an amber stream at a decaying stump.

"You ain't—" he paused and almost whispered the word, "*heard* nothin' up there nights, have ya?"

As clearly as though it had happened within the hour, I can remember the quick glances we shot at one another, and the sudden, chill breath that stirred at the back of my neck as we asked him why.

"Guess you're the first fellers that's slept there for fifteen years," he said, and I fancied there was a hint of respect in his voice. "Yes, sir, the crew up and moved right after the murder."

"Murder!"

"Yeah. You must o' heard tell of it. There was a teamster murdered there when they was strippin' this lot. Some kind of a drunken row over a woman. Feller's name was Payson. He'd just opened the door and was goin' in after his hosses when the chopper let him have it with an ax. Split his head open clear down to his chin. You musta read about it."

I hadn't—and quite suddenly in the back of my mind I could feel the conviction being born that I wished I had also never heard about it. The story in itself was nothing. It did not matter—much—that the sun had set, that twilight was falling, and that night was only a matter of minutes away. The important thing was that it was something which had really happened—and within thirty feet of the spot where we proposed to sleep for the night.

It may be I shall forget that evening sometime, but if I

ever do there will not be much left that I can recall. I remember that we watered the horse earlier than usual, that
we strained the halter a bit tighter and saw to it that the log
rested evenly and firmly against the closed door. I think,
too, that we talked more than was our usual custom as we
prepared supper, and laughed loudly at our own jokes, but
quite frequently there would be a break in the conversation,
and a brooding and unnatural silence would settle over us
for a moment as we listened to the trickle of water from the
spring, and the sighing of the night wind among the
branches.

The lantern flame was guttering for want of oil ere we
began preparing for bed, but the blankets had not yet en-
folded us when at once we were all frozen into startled immobility as the sound of something moving just outside the
tent came to our ears. I really think it should be recorded
to our credit that we went outside at once. That we emerged
as a single unit, bristling with guns like an armored tank,
does not matter. It is the fact that we went out that counts.

A dark bulk loomed before us; a second glance assured
us that it was the horse, standing close beside the tent, as
though for want of companionship. We went in and filled
the lantern, making a three-boy job of it and spilling a little
oil, I fear, and then lighted it and came out to see what light
it would shed on the affair. The horse was halterless. We

found the halter in the shed, tied as we had tied it, but with the throat latch drawn from its leather loop and unbuckled as neatly as though by human hands. The door creaked on its rusty hinges, the eight-foot log that we had propped so carefully against it lay a few feet away, but there was no telltale mark in the earth to show that it had been pushed there by the pressure of the horse against the inner side of the door.

We discuss it sometimes now when the three of us chance to meet, but, although we have considered it from every angle, it is a problem which we have never solved. Sometimes I think the farmer was rigging us, and that the whole thing was a practical joke on his part—and then I recall that, unsophisticated though he was, there was a look of intelligence about him; and certainly no intelligent person would have tried a thing like that so near to three wide-eyed youngsters whose guns were within arms' reach, and who were as quick on the trigger as we.

There are yet two other things about it which still linger in my memory. I recall that I slept fitfully that night, and that we pulled the tent down quite early the next morning, foregoing another day of guaranteed shooting, and moving on to other and unexplored fields.

Without being the least bit vainglorious, I do take a small measure of credit to myself for learning to shoot with some degree of accuracy at grouse and woodcock, but to more than any other man in the world I am indebted to Herb, for no one may be intimately associated with a master of any art without absorbing some of the qualities that make him great. He could not only bring in more birds than any other man of my acquaintance, but he could kill bird after bird that got up underfoot, in cover so thick that he had to shoot quickly or not at all, and not more than once in a hundred times would he render a bird unfit for table purposes. Nothing delighted me more than to watch him shoot, and I am sure nothing ever made my own efforts seem so futile, for while I was devoting every energy to the task of centering my bird, he calmly shot at the edge of his and brought it down with a few pellets from the outer fringe of the pattern. On dozens of different occasions when the bird went hurtling past him at a distance of hardly that many feet, I have seen him remove their heads cleanly without placing a single shot in the body, and he could do it with the same ease and unconcern that characterized all his shooting. I thought then that I could never begin to approach his uncanny skill, and time has proven how right I was in my estimation of my powers; but he helped me immeasurably, for he set a pattern which I have ever since tried to follow.

Probably it is entirely a matter of psychology, but as it

was proven to me when I made my glaring error on that first flock of geese, it bolsters up some mental weakness when one picks out the exact spot he wishes to hit. All too frequently the bird hunter must shoot entirely by instinct, but I learned after a weary while to shoot at one wing of those birds which would have been ruined by a center shot, and I have occasionally executed the more difficult feat of decapitation, but I can do it no longer. It requires the keen, sharp-focusing vision of youth for frills of that sort, and now on an exceptionally close bird I hold well above it if it be a rising one, or well ahead of a cross shot, and trust that the lesser number of pellets which come stringing along behind will get there at the right time. They do occasionally, but all too frequently they do not.

It is hard to overcome the habits and practices of a lifetime, but if I were beginning again, I think I would school myself to pass up those shots which must be taken at a distance of less than thirty feet. Game was never plentiful enough to warrant the waste of even a single specimen, and most certainly it is not now. Quite frequently when a fellow is doing his very best he will no more than rake a close bird with the edge of the charge, but all too often it is a direct hit, and that bit of bird life has been utterly wasted. It is far better to let the bird go for a distance of fifteen yards, or, if that is not possible, to refrain from shooting at all.

Similarly, anyone who shoots at birds beyond a reasonable range is only hurting his own sport, for even one shot lodged in the intestines is quite certain ultimately to cause death, although some prowling fox or skunk will be the only one to profit thereby. Most grouse are killed at ranges between fifteen and thirty-five yards, the latter being about the safe maximum distance for a cylinder or modified choke, for despite the occasional lucky shot that might seem to prove the reverse to be true, a ruffed grouse is capable of carrying off quite a bit of lead. No one can say how many pellets are necessary to stop it in mid-air, for the nerve centers they touch and the bones they break are the deciding factors, but I have seen many a hard-hit bird travel fast and far before it came to earth.

Only last fall, within a few days of the end of the season, I had that fact brought home to me in an unpleasant manner. Grouse had been relatively scarce, but up in the foothills we had found a few places where they were plentiful enough so that we felt we could take a few without suffering any pangs of conscience.

The country was particularly open, and most of the chances were farther than I like to have them. It was that, coupled with the fact that the birds had their full winter plumage, which induced me to use No. 7½ chilled rather than the 9's which I prefer earlier in the season.

For two days they worked out as nicely as one could wish. We missed some birds we should have killed, but on the other hand we killed some we should have missed, and these latter, added to those we should have killed and did, gave us a satisfying total. Then, late in the afternoon and over a staunch point, a bird broke exactly as I had planned she should. It was a perfect cross shot, with hardly a tree to hinder, and the distance was not over twenty-five yards. It was the kind of a shot a blind man would welcome, and as I touched the trigger I knew that I was right and that the bird's moment had come. I could see the feathers flick upward as the shot lifted them along her back, and they puffed away from her in a thousand tiny fragments, but although she flinched mightily at the impact she kept steadily on. I was so sure that the next wing beat would be her last that I withheld the second shot for an instant, and then I saw her body tilt just the least bit downward as she continued her headlong flight.

Forty yards away, and directly before her, a rounded knoll arose, rock-studded and scoured by the storms of centuries, until not so much as a bush grew upon it. From her angle of flight I could tell it was going to be a mighty close thing if she made it over the top. I had ample time to loose another charge at her, and a reasonably good chance of connecting with it, but while I did not wish her any more bad luck than had befallen her in the last few moments, if she was destined to crack up among those boulders, I had an overmastering desire to witness it.

She cleared it only by inches, between two jutting bits of rock, and disappeared instantly beyond the brow of the knoll. Calling the dog over from where he still held rigidly, I followed her course over the ridge, fully expecting to find her within a distance of fifty yards from it.

We were still looking for her some ten minutes later, when I heard a distant hail from my companion. I called him over and explained the situation and for an hour thereafter the two of us, with a pair of dogs, combed that country back and forth as carefully as though we were hunting for a lost dime, but not a trace of her could we find. I knew when I pulled the trigger that I was holding correctly, and I knew an instant later by the almost imperceptible shift of balance in her body, that the bird was dead. After it attains the speed and altitude it desires, the normal flight of a ruffed grouse is not accomplished by an uninterrupted series of wing beats, but is a soaring glide interspersed with brief moments when the power is turned on with a wide-open throttle; but this bird's wings had not ceased their driving thrust even after she had started the gradual descent which must eventually bring her back to earth.

I disliked leaving her there, for I would far rather come

home empty-handed than with the memory of a wounded
bird or animal that managed to get away; but although we
swung wide at last and searched the more distant and less
likely places, we were obliged to acknowledge defeat.

"I guess you didn't hurt her very bad," my companion
said. "A stray shot or two through the feathers. If she had
come down the dogs would have found her."

It would have eased my conscience considerably if I
could have believed him, but when I tried to do so, I found
it impossible. The memory interrupted my slumber that
night, and the next day it kept intruding upon my mind, at
the most unexpected moments, until I could stand it no
longer. We were five miles from the spot, but I stopped and
turned to my companion.

"It's no use," I told him. "I've got to go back and find
that bird we lost yesterday."

He is the sort of chap with whom I like to hunt, for he
understood my feelings and readily agreed. We drove over,
left the car and worked our way up to the spot. The scene
was still fresh in my mind, and I could accurately recall the
bird's line of flight. With the dogs ranging closely before
us we started over the brow of the hill, and kept on and on
until my companion's judgment caused him to remonstrate.

"Dead or alive, she would never have come this far," he
said, and it seemed reasonable, for we were more than two

hundred yards from the spot where I last saw her; but scores of similar happenings had made me obstinate.

"This was the direction she took," I insisted, "and she was a dead bird. She could not voluntarily change her course."

We went on again, making the dogs range close and carefully. Fifty yards farther along my dog slowed suddenly and came to a half-hearted point. Just ahead of him a few scrubby and wind-battered young pines struggled valiantly for existence, and though I knew it was a likely place for a grouse to be hiding, just at that moment I was not interested in live birds.

"Go fetch," I ordered; and the dog went in and came out with the bird, her head and neck outstretched as they had been when I last saw them, her wings still rigidly spread to their fullest extent.

We dissected her on the spot. A few pellets had creased the skin along her back and had been responsible for the cloud of feathers left floating behind her, but there were three shot holes in the lower portion of her breast—and five more well grouped in the center of her body. The latter were far enough ahead so that they had passed directly through her vitals. A more minute examination disclosed the fact that one pellet had almost severed her heart, while three more had made a sorry mess of her liver; but she had

[ 222 ]

flown not an inch less than 250 yards beyond the spot where she had been when I pulled the trigger.

Generally speaking, a rising bird is easier to bring to earth than one which has achieved the required velocity and is gliding along with set wings. Under the latter circumstance it is almost imperative either to break bones or to paralyze whatever nerve center it is that controls the bird's equilibrium. It is for that reason that I prefer shot of a finer size than most people recommend. With two pellets in a bird instead of one, the chance of breaking a bone is exactly doubled; and no one need worry about the penetration of even No. 10 chilled, if there is a fairly stiff load of powder behind it and the distance is not greater than thirty-five yards. I have killed many black ducks with loads of that kind, when I have jumped them from brooks while hunting woodcock, and none of them have exhibited any hesitancy about dying. I recall a morning when a distant bombardment drew me down through the woods to the river, where I found a chap shooting mergansers that were coming in from the ocean to feed. He was a veritable giant of a man, and he was armed with a 10-gauge Richards double that must have weighed at least ten pounds. He had a well-constructed blind, a backload of decoys and silhouettes, and he was doing a land-office business.

Despite the size of the weapon, his own stature was so

colossal that he was not overarmed, but I had entered that experimental period of my life when I was searching for something of feather-lightness that would still be effective, and I was carrying a 20-gauge double. I had a pocketful of shells but they were all woodcock loads of three-fourths of an ounce of No. 10 soft shot.

I do not remember who started the argument, but I suppose it was inevitable, for each of us was firm in his conviction that the other was a crack-brained idiot. I insisted that all cannons should be mounted on some form of gun carriage. He maintained that my five-and-a-half pound weapon would not kill humming birds regularly at a distance of thirty feet. It ended by his moving over and inviting me to occupy the blind with him and make good my boasting. I accepted with alacrity, and never has fortune smiled more benignly upon me than it did that morning.

We shot alternately, irrespective of whether the ducks came singly or in flocks, and in an hour's time I had folded up seven birds without a miss, while he had accounted for only five, although he had had several more opportunities for doubles than I.

He would not believe the evidence of his eyes until he had cut open one of my shells, but then he apologized handsomely, giving all credit to the little gun and never once suspecting the real cause of my success.

[ 224 ]

The blind was located about fifty yards above a bend in the river, and as the ducks swept around it at full speed their momentum carried them well in toward our hide-out. It was strategically located, but I am sure he placed it there more through accident than design, for he did not know how to profit by the advantage it gave him. Because of his excessive bulk his movements were slow and cumbersome, and he invariably shoved out a foot or more of those gigantic gunbarrels before the birds were within range. They would see it instantly, and although the speed at which they were travelling carried them well up toward him, they nevertheless were banking sharply upward when he shot. My years on the marshes had taught me to hug the blind tightly, without movement, until the moment when the birds were just where I wished them to be, and then to go after them as fast as I went after rising grouse. By following the latter method on that memorable morning, I shot at not one duck which was more than thirty-five yards distant from me, and some of them were scarcely half that—and no duck can fly through the center of the pattern of even No. 10's at that distance and emerge in good physical condition.

Some years ago a trapshooting friend of mine went down to the seashore for his first try at coot shooting. Locating their battery off a jutting point, he and his companion were just in time to engage in hostilities with an exceptionally heavy flight of loons that were travelling southward. My friend came back empty-handed, but with the weird story that he had repeatedly heard the unmistakable thud as a charge of No. 4 shot landed on the body of a loon that was well within range, with no other result than to elicit a mirthful chuckle from the amused creature. He was convinced, he assured me, that nothing smaller than B.B.'s would penetrate their inch-thick armorplate of feathers, and not even then if the bird presented a head-on or a broadside shot.

I contended that if he ever centered one at thirty-five yards with No. 4's he would have a dead loon to dispose of, but he ridiculed the idea, and there we let the matter rest.

Two weeks later I motored down for a week-end with the ducks on the old marshes, and as I rounded an abrupt bend in the river on the first morning, I saw a full-grown loon sitting on the water at a distance of approximately thirty-five yards. Not since my boyhood days had I destroyed life wantonly, but our argument was still fresh in my mind; therefore I leveled the gun at the bird and pulled the trigger. Death was so instantaneous that the stricken loon did not even flutter, but flattened out on the water as though struck by a lightning bolt. An accommodating east wind kicked it ashore, and I proceeded at once to skin it. When I unrolled it two days later, and spread it on a table before my friend so that he might see the shot holes which more than twenty-five No. 6 pellets had made as they entered; and when I had pointed out where they were still embedded in the skin on the opposite side, he, too, admitted the truth of the old adage that, "To err is human."

The surest way to grass any bird is to break its wing. The next-best method is to place a shot pellet in the head or the vertebrae of the spinal column. The third most effective thing is to get two or more shot through the flat bones of the back. A broken-winged bird may be hard to find without a dog—and oftentimes with one—but the other two will not travel after they hit the ground.

On the other hand, a bird with only one shot through the fleshy part of the body may come tumbling down dead —or another with a half dozen pellets apparently similarly placed may fly an incredible distance before it succumbs. I prefer to break bones, and for that reason I shall continue to shoot 9's until the season is well advanced, after which I may or may not change to 7½'s. It will depend largely upon the way the birds are lying. If the majority of them get up within thirty yards of me, I have no cause to worry. If they rise beyond that distance, they have none, no matter what size of shot I use, for the good old business of snap shooting does not work out so well on long shots unless they chance to be straightaways. With me at least, the matter of leading my bird is something which I have worked out subconsciously. My mind takes care of it automatically on all cross shots at short or medium ranges, but I have schooled myself so rigorously to pass up the longer ones, that when I do choose to take one the shutter clicks just an instant too soon.

It no longer frets me, however. I hunt grouse for the thrill it gives me, and I get infinitely more from maneuvering either the bird or myself into a position where I can get a close, sure shot, than I would in squinting along the barrel and killing half a dozen of them at fifty yards.

Unless a fellow specializes in that type of shooting, it is almost criminal to shoot at birds at extremely long ranges, and even then he should not do so unless accompanied by a capable retriever. Good retrievers, moreover, are almost as scarce among pointers and setters as are good grouse dogs, if I may judge from those over which I have hunted. In all my life I have intimately known only three dogs who were real top-notchers at finding crippled game.

No one will question the fact that a dead bird is often a hard one to find. I have often seen dogs which were widely acknowledged to be good retrievers, pass directly over a lifeless grouse or woodcock, and in one or two instances actually step on it, without being in the least aware of its proximity. Such birds can be found if the dog works his ground slowly and in some degree systematically, although I will forgive him if he occasionally fails; but the dog who loses a wounded and running grouse deserves all the opprobrium that the irate owner heaps upon his head.

By a strange coincidence, the three good retrievers were of different breeds, but it was no coincidence that their manner of locating their quarry was the same. When a hasty search disclosed the fact that the bird was not where they had seen it fall, each of the three had the brains to put his nose to the ground, circle until he picked up the track, and then follow it as a hound trails.

The first of the three was my own black-and-white spaniel. The fact that he followed foot scent was not to his credit, for it was the natural spaniel method, but nevertheless he was good at it. On several different occasions while hunting over another dog, I went home for him when we had a bird down and were unable to find it, and although once or twice I put him down on a trail that was hours old, he would take it and bound away, to return in a few moments with the prize.

On one occasion, while tending a line of mink traps, a pair of blue-wing teal came swinging up the river toward me. I downed one with each barrel, but the first bird suffered no more than a broken wing, and swam the short distance to the bank and disappeared over it before I could reload. I was nearly a mile from home, but I went back and called the dog. In order to get across the river it was necessary to travel yet another mile to a bridge, which we did and came back to where the dead bird still floated in the sluggish current. The dog retrieved it, and then I took him to the spot where the other one had come out upon the bank. He took the trail at a pace which called for the best there was in me to follow. We went through a short strip of pasture land, then across a broad field, and came at last to the edge of the crescent of woods which fringed the marshes. I never knew until then how keen was a duck's sense of direction, for I doubt if it deviated a hundred feet from a straight line, nor did it do so on the way through the woods. Out upon the marsh the dog went, and was lost to my view among the tall grasses, but as I hurried along in the trail he had made, I met him returning with the bird in his mouth. It may be that I am prejudiced, but I still think it was fine retrieving, for the trail was more than an hour old, and it was almost three-quarters of a mile long.

The second dog was a pointer, a high-headed, body-scent dog, but when occasion demanded it he could put his nose to the ground and trail a broken-winged grouse with the best of them. I have written about him before, but the story is so good that I feel it will bear repeating, for as an exhibition of stamina and grit, of indomitable will and all

[ 230 ]

the unquenchable fires that go to make up a good dog, I have never witnessed its equal.

It was late October, and Vaughn and I were shooting ducks on the river. The weather was cold, and a nasty northeaster was kicking up a sea that drove hundreds of ducks in to the shelter of the marshes.

Vaughn had taken the pointer along, for he was one of the very few of his breed that would retrieve equally well from water or land. We had downed a few which he brought in, only to lie shivering and shaking in true pointer fashion, but alert and waiting for the next victim to strike the water.

Then a sheldrake came down with a broken wing. It dived instantly, but when it came up it was well out of range—and the dog was out there after it. The tide was running out strongly, and the speed of the dog and duck was so great that, hurrying along the shore behind them, we were hard pressed to keep up. Then a creek which was too deep to wade intervened, and we were forced into a detour that cost us several precious minutes. When we caught sight of them again they were just entering the maelstrom of water on the bar.

Unless one has witnessed it he cannot imagine the tremendous power of the tumbling waves and cross currents that beat upon the shallow ridge of sand at the river's mouth when the storm gods have unloosed their wrath. A rowboat would be crushed like an eggshell, and a man would be a strong swimmer indeed who could win through it without being battered into insensibility, but the dog was there in the midst of it, beaten and hammered incessantly about, lost to our view for long moments at a time as a wave bore him under, but rising again to fight onward toward the bird that danced and skittered like a bobbing cork before him.

I have seen dogs who possessed the courage to hunt all day on feet that were cut and bleeding. I have seen them go on and on unflinchingly through thorn bushes and brier patches when the thin skin of their legs was inflamed and swollen, but I have never seen another in whom high courage flamed so strongly as it did in that slashing pointer of the long ago.

So powerful was the wind and the tumult of the sea that I suppose he did not hear our frenzied cries to him to come back, but I know now that he would not have heeded them even though he had heard, for the bird was there before him and there was work yet to be done.

Had it not been for the force of the tide behind him, I am sure that he would never have won his way through the mad vortex, but he did, and was presently fighting his way out into the broad Atlantic. Side by side, Vaughn and I stood on the shore, silent now because of the great awe that filled our hearts, and watched the bobbing head grow even smaller as the distance between us increased, until it was blotted out at last by the spindrift that scudded before the flailing wind.

Both wind and tide had conspired to influence the fleeing duck to choose a southerly direction—and we were on the north side of the river. It was preposterous to expect the dog's body would drift ashore for days, but actuated by the faint hope that some fluke of air or ocean current might bear it back to us, we hurried two miles up the river to a bridge, crossed it, and came back again on the other side, to stand presently upon the sand hummocks which flanked the beach, and stare hopelessly out across the white capped and storm tossed ocean.

The dog had been so far away when I last saw him that my gaze was focused upon the smoky horizon, while I hoped against hope that I might catch a glimpse of his seal-brown head, when Vaughn's incredulous and mighty shout rang in my ears.

"By God! There's my dog!"

He was gone instantly, running like a man possessed down across the sands of the beach toward the water's edge, and looking that way I saw the glorious animal fighting in through the breakers, spent, but with his irresistible fire still unquenched—and with the duck, alive, in his mouth.

[ 233 ]

The other great retriever was my friend's setter, to whom I may already have allotted too much space, but never too much praise. I can see him now in fancy, a flash of glittering white as he bounded in after a bird, and then, bothered for a moment, put his nose to the ground and cast off in ever-widening circles until he found the trail. He had almost a thousand woodcock and grouse killed over him, in all sorts of cover, but he never once failed to bring in the bird if it came to earth within our view, and he brought in dozens of them that we had no idea were hit.

Most dogs have a natural inclination to retrieve, but only the gifted ones will become great. All may be helped though, by staying with them and lending them one's moral assistance and support until the bird is found, but I believe it is bad practice to direct the dog too closely, even though you chance to know where the victim is lying. The more assistance one gives, the more he will be depended upon to do so—and the man has done his share of the work when he kills the game. It is the dog's job to find it.

Among prospectors there is a saying that "Silver is in the high places and gold is where you find it." With only a slight modification, the axiom might be applied to ruffed grouse and woodcock, for while the latter often wanders into all sorts of places, the feeding and nesting grounds of the former are as fixed as the course of the stars.

If bird-sense is an essential requisite in a dog, it most certainly should be cultivated by a hunter; yet it is surprising how many men depend upon someone else to lead them around to spots which birds frequent. I suppose some men have more "feeling" for a birdy bit of country than others, but it has always seemed to me that it is more a matter of observation and memory than anything else, for when a fellow comes to a place that is exactly similar to a hundred others in which he has found birds, he is a dull scholar indeed if the connection is not apparent.

The fact was demonstrated to me quite forcibly only a few months ago. Our woodcock flight occurred much later than usual last fall, and instead of their beginning to drift in about the middle of October as is their usual custom, I saw no signs of migrating birds until the season had closed. Shortly thereafter, a friend of mine who does not hunt, came to me with the information that on the previous day he had started several of the birds while walking through a strip of woods not more than half a mile from my home. The far places have ever seemed the fairest to me, and for that reason I had not entered that territory for several years, although I knew it had harbored a few birds at one time. Slipping a camera in my pocket, I called the dog and we started out, for I was anxious to have my neighbor get the thrill of seeing a dog on an intense point.

[ 235 ]

The woods had changed since I last saw them, and I had not the slightest idea where we would find the birds, and neither, it presently developed, did my friend, for although he had seen them less than twenty-four hours previously, he had no recollection of what part of the cover he had been in at the time.

We scoured the territory for something like twenty minutes without the dog once showing any indication of gaminess, and then, off to our left, I noticed a low birch-crowned knoll. I did not remember then, nor do I recall now, that I had ever killed a bird there, but all at once I knew that if there were any birds in the cover, that was where we would find them.

I said something to that effect as I swung toward it and motioned the dog on, and my judgment was vindicated almost at once, for I snapped a roll of films and flushed six woodcock from under the dog's nose in less than ten minutes, from a patch of ground that comprised not more than an eighth of an acre.

My friend would have been no more overwhelmed had I rolled up my sleeves and extracted the birds one by one from my hat, for he claimed I was possessed of some sinister, black magic, but it was nothing more than the faint echo within my consciousness of scores of other situations which were almost exactly similar.

In like manner, every good gunner has learned to profit by observation. The fox hunter will climb a hill in country which is entirely new to him, look over the surrounding landscape and say: "The old boy will cross that thar knoll sometime before dark," and he is quite likely to be right. The deer hunter will follow the same procedure, and say: "Down there in that valley is where we will find our deer." And a grouse hunter, sitting beside you as you tool the old bus along a rutted and unknown road, will suddenly grasp your arm and cry: "Whoa! Hold on! Boy! Look at that corner! That sure looks *good!*"

I knew one setter that followed the same line of reasoning whenever we visited a certain cover. In it were two large and prolific old apple trees, and frequently there was a grouse or two feeding beneath each of them. After a time we noticed that the dog would always slow up as we came to them, then creep stealthily ahead and freeze into a solid point, but we soon learned he was doing it only on general principles. It was a likely place in which to find a bird, and he wished to apprise us of the fact. He fooled us many a time, but I always liked him, for while his nose was wholly undependable, he had an ample supply of grey matter, and gave me many a treasure to store in my vault of memories.

I open it occasionally and pore over my assembled wealth, for if there is any consolation in being a forty-niner

I most certainly find it there. My days are yet too full for retrospection, but at night when the fire has burned low and the whispering silence comes, I pause, as I have paused on this occasion, to live again the days of a golden past.

I find, as I review them, that I have little cause for regret. Generations as yet unborn will thrill to joys that are beyond my comprehension—but my heartbeat has quickened to the thunder of such multitudes of rising grouse as they may never know.

Cradled in the fastness of a rugged wilderness, inured alike to winter's icy blasts and summer's tropic sun, I believe the ruffed grouse has the wile and courage and stamina to continue to perpetuate his species. I hope I am right, for while the woodlands still call me with all their old allure, I can picture a no more desolate scene than one in which the last old drummer has beat his last rolling tattoo.

The years have been many since I crowned him king, but he has never tottered upon his throne, and I still accord him all homage and respect. My one regret is that he may never know the measure of my esteem; and that although I hope to joust with him for many years to come, and match my wit against his in a game where oblivion is the penalty he must pay for a mistake, I do it only because I love him.

"The king is dead. Long live the king!"